A Passion for Glass

A Passion

for Glass

The Aviva and Jack A. Robinson

Studio Glass Collection

Bonita Fike

THE DETROIT INSTITUTE OF ARTS

COVER:
PAUL MANNERS, *Pythias* (no. 42), 1986, detail

TITLE PAGE:
DOMINICK LABINO, *Untitled* from the
Emergence series (no. 31), 1974, detail

The Robinsons dedicate this book to
their children and grandchildren.

This catalogue is published in conjunction with the exhibition
"A Passion for Glass: The Aviva and Jack A. Robinson Studio
Glass Collection" at the Detroit Institute of Arts, October 11,
1998–February 14, 1999.

The exhibition was organized by the Detroit Institute of Arts and
is made possible with the support of Aviva and Jack A. Robinson,
the Michigan Council for Arts and Cultural Affairs, and the City
of Detroit.

ISBN: 0-89558-150-7

Director of Publications: Julia P. Henshaw
Editor: Maya Hoptman
Director of Visual Resources: Dirk Bakker
Design: Julie Pincus, Birmingham, Michigan

Distributed by Antique Collectors Club, Wappingers Falls, N.Y., and
Woodbridge, Suffolk, England

Printed by University Lithoprinters, Inc., Ann Arbor, Michigan

Library of Congress Cataloging-in-Publication Data

Fike, Bonita, 1946-
    A passion for glass : the Aviva and Jack A. Robinson studio glass collec-
    tion / Bonita Fike.
        p.   cm.
    Published in conjunction with an exhibition at the Detroit Institute of
Arts, Oct. 11, 1998-Feb. 14, 1999.
    Includes bibliographical references.
    ISBN 0-89558-150-7
    1. Art glass—United States—History—20th century—Exhibitions.
2. Robinson, Aviva—Art collections—Exhibitions. 3. Robinson, Jack A.
(Jack Albert), 1930- —Art collections—Exhibitions. 4. Art glass—Private
collections—Michigan—Detroit—Exhibitions. 5. Art glass—Michigan—
Detroit—Exhibitions. 6. Detroit Institute of Arts—Exhibitions. I. Detroit
Institute of Arts. II. Title.
NK5112.F45 1998
748.2913'09'04507477434—dc21   98-38669
                                                CIP

Contents

Director's Foreword and Acknowledgments

The philanthropic tradition of building new collections by means of gifts from magnanimous donors in the Detroit community has been continued by Aviva and Jack A. Robinson, who have donated their impressive studio glass collection, numbering seventy-eight pieces, to the museum. In addition, they have endowed a gallery for the display of twentieth-century decorative arts and design objects. Combined with the existing holdings, the gift will enable the Detroit Institute of Arts to present the evolution of this fascinating medium for our visitors, including the general public, collectors, glassmakers, students, and educators. It is a valuable community resource in a region that has a national reputation for studio glass production, education, and collecting. We are greatly indebted to Aviva and Jack Robinson for helping us to realize this important aspect of the museum's mission.

The first studio glass pieces to enter the museum were a gift in 1970 from Mr. and Mrs. Walter E. Simmons. An appropriate foundation for the collection, these six works are by Dominick Labino, who, with Harvey Littleton, is credited with founding the studio glass movement in 1962. In 1980 and 1981 collector and scholar Jean Sosin with her husband Hilbert Sosin helped expand the holdings through their donation of eleven glass objects by John Lewis, Charles Lotton, James Lundberg, John Nygren, and Sylvia Vigiletti. Since 1987, Joan and Bernard Chodorkoff have generously given twenty-seven pieces from their extensive collection of more than one hundred, which is promised to the DIA in memory of their son David Jacob Chodorkoff. The remaining twenty-one works in the museum's holdings were either gifts or were purchased with funds from the local community.

The Robinsons' decision to make their gift to the DIA resulted from discussions with three former executives of the museum: Samuel Sachs II, director; Joseph P. Bianco, Jr., executive vice president of the Founders Society; and Jan van der Marck, chief curator and curator of Twentieth-Century Art. We are much indebted to associate curator Bonita Fike, who organized this exhibition and wrote the catalogue, and to her colleagues in the Department of Twentieth-Century Art, curator MaryAnn Wilkinson and curatorial coordinator Rebecca Hart, who provided essential advice and assistance during the course of this project. Julie Pincus's design for the catalogue is not only handsome, but evocative of the very works of art it presents. Our thanks go to Ferdinand Hampson and Lillian Zonars of Habatat Galleries; Ferd provided the insightful catalogue introduction, and Lillian gave invaluable assistance in the documentation of the artists' careers.

Many dedicated members of the staff worked on the exhibition, including group director of exhibitions and design Louis Gauci, who took a large gallery that was interrupted by four large openings and a multilevel ceiling and created an eloquent and unified space to display the glass works. Dirk Bakker, director of visual resources, is responsible for the admirable photographs reproduced in the catalogue. He was assisted by museum volunteer Alice Hoffer, who spent endless hours coordinating the photographs, slides, and transparencies. Julia Henshaw, director of publications, provided editorial expertise and guidance, and associate editor Maya Hoptman contributed her editorial skills to the success of the catalogue. Collections manager Terry Birkett supervised the renovation of a storeroom to house the works, and museum technician James Fuqua oversaw the challenging issues of storage and provided art-handling expertise throughout the project. Conservator of sculpture and decorative arts Carol Forsythe carefully prepared the glass for exhibition, and mount designer and fabricator James Leacock created the installation mounts. Research assistant Cheryl La Pat is to be commended for her help with many aspects of the exhibition.

Performing arts coordinator Rudy Lauerman and audio-visual technicians Kiersten Armstrong and Seth Kirk consulted with Herb Babcock, artist and professor at the Center for Creative Studies (CCS), College of Art and Design, Detroit, on an innovative computer touch-screen program that shows Babcock, CCS instructor Theresa Pierzchala, and artist Cristen Velliky demonstrating three different glassmaking techniques which were employed in the making of objects in the exhibition. Assistant education curators Gina Alexander-Granger and Stephanie James thoughtfully coordinated the production of labels and gallery sheets as well as the planning of public lectures and classes. Education studio manager Lisa Blackburn organized a children's workshop and an educators' afternoon.

And, lastly, our profound gratitude goes to Aviva and Jack Robinson, who kindly gave of their time, answering numerous questions and attending many meetings. In addition to their generosity, their patience, good humor, and enthusiasm have fortified us all.

Maurice D. Parrish
Interim Director
The Detroit Institute of Arts

An Appreciation

One of the outstanding features of the history of art in our century has been the blurring of the traditional boundaries between the various media. Paintings have become three dimensional, appropriating the aspects of sculpture; sculptures are often incised, tending toward drawing; and nowhere is there a more complete fusion of the elements of art than in glass. Modern studio glass knows no boundaries, and color, form, line, and substance all join to become a new world of expression unto itself.

No collectors seem to have appreciated this more than Aviva and Jack Robinson. Aviva, a master watercolor artist, has perhaps more reason to intuitively gravitate to the field of studio glass. Jack brings a photographer's eye and an analytical mind to the appreciation of glass.

Modern philanthropy has no better exemplars than Aviva and Jack. Theirs is the understanding that encompasses not only the educational value of their gift to future generations of musuem visitors and curators alike, but also the value their gift brings to the city of their birth in terms of recognition and leadership in the visual arts. Detroit is now, by dint of their generosity, instantly a major center for the study of studio glass.

As former director, I welcome this opportunity to salute the Robinsons for their most significant contribution in building the collection of twentieth-century art.

Samuel Sachs II
Director, The Frick Collection
New York

The Collectors:
Aviva and Jack A. Robinson

The year 1995 ended on a joyful note at the Detroit Institute of Arts thanks to the generosity of Aviva and Jack Robinson. A donation of seventy-eight works from their outstanding studio glass collection more than doubled the museum's holdings of contemporary glass.

The Robinsons' interest in studio glass began in the 1970s when the movement was in its infancy, and they continue to actively acquire today. Thanks to their enthusiasm for the daring and experimental, the collection virtually represents a history of the development of studio glass. Aviva said, "The Detroit Institute of Arts is a treasure, and we could think of no more appropriate home for our glass treasures."[1]

This donation was accompanied by a second major gift: in order to support the exhibition of contemporary crafts, the Robinsons have generously endowed the 2,400-square-foot central gallery of the Twentieth-Century Art suite. And what could be more appropriate as the first exhibition in the newly refurbished gallery than "A Passion for Glass: The Aviva and Jack A. Robinson Studio Glass Collection"? After the exhibition closes, the Robinson Gallery will be used to display a wide variety of decorative arts and design objects of the twentieth century.

The sparkle, translucence, and brilliant color of contemporary glass combine to elicit a broad array of visual responses, a factor that makes it attractive to Aviva and Jack. They are fascinated by the material as well as the ideas being expressed. The Robinsons have always been pleased to share their enthusiasm and what they have learned about glass, often hosting groups in their beautiful home. Designed to focus attention on their art collection, the house, situated on a lake, has floor-to-ceiling windows that allow light, in all its changing intensities, to flood the rooms, illuminating the works of art (see fig. 1).

Around 1985 they began to realize that not only was their collection an educational tool, providing a chronological overview of contemporary studio glass, but also that many of the individual works were of museum quality. Given their devotion to learning and their commitment to the community, they decided to donate their collection to the DIA. Jack explained, "We were both born and raised in Detroit. We have always lived and earned our living in Detroit. We never considered any other institution."

The Robinsons are involved in a number of philanthropic causes, including United Way Community Services, the United Jewish Foundation, and Harper Hospital. Jack has recently been named chairman of the Policy Committee of the Southeastern Michigan Community Partnership for Cultural Participation, a committee of the Community Foundation for Southeastern Michigan. Their dedication to the arts led them to take an active role in Concerned Citizens for the Arts in Michigan, of which Jack is former chairman, and in the DIA, where Aviva is a trustee and member of the Modern Decorative Arts Group, a committee of the Friends of Modern Art.

Aviva and Jack were the first in their families to graduate from college: Jack with a degree in pharmacy and Aviva one in art education, both from Wayne State University in Detroit. They met on a blind date when Aviva was a seventeen-year-old high school student and Jack was twenty and in college. A year after they were married in 1952, Jack was drafted. When he returned from two years of service in the U.S. Army, he went to work as a pharmacist. The Robinsons opened the first Perry Drug Store in 1957 on the corner of Perry Street and East Boulevard in Pontiac, Michigan, using $200 of their own money and borrowing the rest. According to Jack, "It was named after Perry Street because in those days neon letters were $75 each, and Robinson was eight letters and Perry only five. So for $225 I sold out the family name, as the story goes." Jack continued to practice pharmacy until about 1964, all the while opening additional stores. Perry Drug Stores went public in 1973 with eighteen stores. By the time the company, listed on the New York Stock Exchange, was acquired by Rite Aid Corporation in 1995, there were 225 stores, making it the largest drug store chain operating in the state.

Aviva, a professional artist specializing in two- and three-dimensional abstract watercolors, has had more than fifteen one-person shows. At the beginning of her career she fabricated jewelry from metal. Her first job was as an assistant teacher in the children's workshops at the DIA. She also taught for a year at Oak Park High School before the first of their three daughters was born in 1955. Even when Shelby, Beth, and Abby were young, she remained involved in art by volunteering as a docent at the DIA. Working in her art studio she became uncomfortable having the materials necessary for making jewelry—acid, solder, and blowtorches—around the children. Instead, she tried watercolor painting and collage and discovered that she truly enjoyed it. In 1966 the Rubiner Gallery in Royal Oak, Michigan, began to represent her work, and in 1972 she had her first one-person show there. She was exclusively represented by the Rubiner Gallery for many years, but also showed at Ward-Nasse and Helen Getler in New York, the Van Straaten Gallery in Chicago, and at Gargoyle in Aspen. The Michigan Watercolor Society Award in 1979, 1980, and 1982 and the Michigan Women's Foundation Award in Painting in 1992 are among the many honors Aviva has received for her art. Her work is in numerous private and corporate collections, including Chrysler Corporate Headquarters in New York, the Ford Motor Company Executive Offices in Dearborn, Michigan, IBM Corporate Headquarters in Armonk, New York, the University of Michigan–Dearborn, and the Detroit Institute of Arts.

Due to Aviva's involvement, the Robinsons' home always contained art, but it was not until 1957 that they acquired their first piece of contemporary glass. It was a gift from her sister of a vase made at the Venini factory in Murano, Italy. Little did the bestower imagine the profound effect it would have on Aviva's art. She was inspired by the transparency, the shifting planes, and intermingling of colors as light passed through the vase, as can be seen in her watercolor collage *Noatak #110* (fig. 2), now in the DIA collection. A later such work, *#101* from her "Circle Series," captures the force of light splitting and refracting colors in the manner of glass. Aviva, with seeming sleight-of-hand, represents the myriad forms that the human eye sees but no camera could ever capture.

Contemporary glass again entered her life in 1971. In that year, Ferdinand Hampson opened Habatat Galleries, the first studio glass gallery in the United States, in Dearborn. Aviva said, "A friend of mine wanted to go to see Ferd's gallery. I went with her. She subsequently lost interest, but I was hooked." Jack's involvement in glass began in 1973 when he accompanied Aviva to view a major purchase she was considering. Jack attributes his interest in glass to Aviva's contagious enthusiasm. The color and form of glass fascinate him, as does its tactile quality: he likes to hold it, to feel its weight. Glass is also enjoyable from a photographer's viewpoint. Jack began taking photographs at the age of ten, and as a teenager he was the class photographer at Detroit's Central High School. Later, he practiced professional photography. "I have photographed the pieces in our collection at different times of the day, and this has been very rewarding for me," he said. Jack experiences glass as both relaxing—he enjoys sitting among the objects and simply contemplating their beauty—and stimulating, in that it has broadened

FIGURE **2**
AVIVA ROBINSON
American, born 1933
Noatak #110, 1981
Watercolor, 69.8 x 91.4 cm (27½ x 36 in.)
Gift of C. Edward and Mary Ellen Wall;
F1984.106

his outlook and philosophy of life and helped him to adapt to the enormous changes in his business career.

Since 1973 the Robinsons have enjoyed collecting together at galleries, fairs, and seminars throughout the world. Most of their works have been acquired through Habatat Galleries, now in Pontiac, but they have also made purchases through the Littleton Gallery in Washington, D.C.; the Robert Kidd Gallery and Yaw Gallery in Birmingham, Michigan; Galeria San Nicola in Venice; and Sanske Gallerie in Zürich, among others. They have met many knowledgeable gallery owners, but Ferd Hampson has been their mentor. Aviva said, "It was a perfect time to collect contemporary glass. Habatat was right here. It was easy. If I had an hour I would run over to Habatat to see what was happening."

The Robinsons have assembled their collection eclectically, driven solely by interest and taste rather than following a particular program or plan. Aviva's aesthetic judgment is central to the process. She is concerned with an object's intrinsic quality: each acquisition represents a personal encounter, and each piece is considered on its own merit. Their first major purchases were in 1985: *Live Oaks and Spanish Moss* (no. 55) by Mark Peiser and *Korallrot Basket Series* (no. 13), a group of nesting bowls by Dale Chihuly, "which we purchased sight unseen at auction, bidding against the Corning Museum of Glass," said Aviva. This piece is of special interest because it was personally blown by Chihuly before a car accident forced him to stop making glass himself. Ferd Hampson said, "When Dale was having these bowls photographed for the cover of the 1978 exhibition guide *Baskets and Cylinders: Recent Glass by Dale*

Chihuly, in order to make the bowls appear more dynamic in the picture, he piled the smaller bowls inside the large bowl. Chihuly liked the effect so much that the *Korallrot Basket Series* became the beginning of his nesting basket series."[2]

Many of the works in the Robinson collection are by Americans, but there are several examples by European artists. The Robinsons felt that in the 1970s and 1980s most of the Europeans were oriented toward factory production and not as creative as American artists. Of the fifty-seven artists represented, fifteen are European, one is Asian, and forty-one are American. The Robinsons purchased their first European piece, *Cylinder Form* (no. 52) by Czech artist Michael Pavlik, in 1978. However, during the last four years almost everything they have acquired has been by European artists, who, influenced by the experimental freedom of American glass art, have been creating exciting pieces. They have collected the work of some artists—including Richard Ritter, Mark Peiser, and Damian Priour—in depth, simply because they like the works. The Robinsons carefully follow the careers of the artists, have met and visited the studios of many, and have invited several to be guests in their home.

In the last thirty years art has become more pluralistic, reflecting the present world culture. The Robinson Collection mirrors this diversity. Just as Aviva's watercolors were prompted by her perceptions of studio glass objects, studio glass has been influenced by the themes and ideas of other fine arts, such as painting, sculpture, and architecture. Writing about a major collection of contemporary art, curator John Beardsley commented, "The difficulty today of putting together a collection of contemporary art that is coherent and yet expressive of diversity is in some ways analogous to a much larger and still unfinished social project—the quest to create a common culture that is tolerant, even respectful, of its various parts. Collecting is one of several ways we might begin to talk about, if not resolve, some of our larger social dilemmas."[3]

Collecting starts with a passion. The Robinsons have that passion: they are willing to take risks, to follow their personal convictions. They continue to collect glass because the artists continue to break new ground. They also have a passion for knowledge and education and realize that objects express something about the time and the place in which they were made. By donating these seventy-eight works to the Detroit Institute of Arts, the Robinsons have made their collection available to all who are interested in this fertile field of artistic expression.

NOTES

1 This essay is based on an interview by Bonita Fike with Aviva and Jack Robinson that took place in September 1997. All quotations, unless otherwise noted, are from the interview.

2 Conversation with Ferdinand Hampson, March 20, 1998. The exhibition was at the Renwick Gallery of the National Museum of American Art, Smithsonian Institution, Washington, D.C., in 1978.

3 New York 1996a, 210.

Introduction

To realize the significance of the Aviva and Jack A. Robinson Studio Glass Collection, we need to reflect on the state of the art in the mid-1970s, when they first made their commitment to this collection. At that time, the most creative artists working in glass were making a living by teaching. Little or no audience for their objects existed; there was only one book on the subject as well as a few austere black-and-white catalogues. Only two galleries in the country regularly displayed these creations, eking out a precarious existence in what seemed to be a disinterested art world. These "artists" would not dare call themselves by such a title, since the art world typically referred to them as craftspeople and often in the most condescending of tones. The collectors of contemporary art considered studio glass to be nothing more than a passing fancy. It was in this environment, that the Robinsons made a commitment—a fearless commitment—to artists using glass as their medium.

I am sure that Jack and Aviva did not get married with the idea of creating the perfect team for collecting contemporary art, but their combined interests achieved this result. The marriage, a loving partnership, brought together all of the right elements necessary to develop a great collection. They share the traits of creativity and sensitivity, and both possess a rare intelligence. But perhaps it is the traits that they do not have in common that have contributed, in a larger measure, to so extraordinary a collection. Aviva, as the artist, is unconventional, emotional. Jack, with a head for business, is the logical thinker, the decision-maker. Together they developed a passion for the glass objects they collected; Aviva with the foresight to recognize the importance of artists stretching the limits of the medium and Jack, perhaps more conservative, yet always keeping an open mind, with his intense interest in learning. I loved to watch as Aviva handily persuaded her reluctant husband into acquiring a particularly adventuresome sculpture, only to have Jack return in a month's time to tell me how much he enjoyed the piece. The ability to stay so open and to learn from the objects is what has made these collectors so unusual. Their fierce commitment gave the artists courage to experiment and discover new possibilities of glass beyond the accomplishments of its nearly 5,000-year history. Aviva and Jack supported artists early in their careers, allowing them the freedom to create and granting them the time to develop and mature as innovative artists—not simply as craftspeople. They have sustained an interest in selecting the best works that they could find and thus have assembled a collection of some of the greatest examples of contemporary glass, whose creators would later be recognized as the premiere artists using this medium. An example of their ability to acquire the seminal work of art was displayed early on, when they purchased a piece by a then little-known artist named Dale Chihuly. The work, titled *Korallrot Basket Series* (no. 13), was the first piece in which Chihuly placed vessels within a vessel to be photographed—a work that launched the career of one of the most celebrated contemporary artists.

Today, due in large part to collectors such as the Robinsons, many artists who work with glass have regular exhibits in prominent museums. Many have books that trace their careers, and critics review their work in noted publications. Hundreds of galleries worldwide vie for a limited number of pieces for an ever-growing collectors' market. The acceleration of interest is virtually unprecedented in the art world. On behalf of all of those who will now have the opportunity to enjoy this great collection at the Detroit Institute of Arts, I would like to thank Jack and Aviva for their outstanding generosity. It is the ultimate gift through which, as collectors, they have demonstrated their support and love for studio glass and for the artists who create in this medium.

Ferdinand C. Hampson
Habatat Galleries
Pontiac, Michigan

The Art-Historical Context of Contemporary Glass

Bonita Fike, Associate Curator of Twentieth-Century Art

Does contemporary glass art speak to the same basic human questions, cultural themes, and historical events that are addressed by such "mainstream" visual arts as painting and sculpture? Can the development of the studio glass movement be seen to parallel that of the other fine arts in the twentieth century?

In order to consider these questions,[1] it is first necessary to turn briefly to the history of the studio glass movement, a term given to the development of small, artist-run studios for the production of art glass beginning in 1962. Interestingly, for most if its roughly 5,000-year history, glass has been made entirely by hand in the setting of a small workshop. It was not until the industrial revolution of the nineteenth century that glass production moved to factories, where its manufacture was much more economical and responsive to the market demand for utilitarian products. Gradually the smaller glassmakers disappeared.

At the beginning of the 1960s, sculptors such as H. C. Westermann and Larry Bell began incorporating glass in their art. However, the glass they used was commercially produced because glassmaking remained beyond the capability of most artists: it requires a high level of technical skill and a large financial investment in equipment. These realities kept production tied to the marketplace. It was an almost universally held assumption that glass, especially blown glass, could only be made successfully in a factory setting.

The transformation of glass from a factory-controlled material to one available for artistic experimentation began in the early 1960s with Harvey Littleton, a professor of ceramics at the University of Wisconsin–Madison. Littleton was born and raised in Corning, New York, where his father was director of research at the Corning Glass Works. He was interested in overcoming the greatest obstacle to artists in producing their own glass: the extremely high temperatures required to melt the ingredients. It was Dominick Labino, vice president and director of research at Johns-Manville Fiber Glass Corporation in Toledo, Ohio, who solved the problem. He developed a type of glass with a lower melting point, which would allow artists working in a studio to use a ceramics kiln as a glass furnace. In 1962 Littleton and Labino demonstrated their discovery at two now-famous workshops at the Toledo Museum of Art. Glass had now become simply another one of the many media from which fine art could be created.

Light, color, and material are one in the medium of glass. Unlike any other medium used to create art, glass allows light to pass through as well as bounce off it; it is totally light-dependent. By passing a beam of light through a prism, the ray breaks (refracts) into the colors of the spectrum: red, orange, yellow, green, blue, and violet. Among the other unique qualities of glass are its optic powers. As a concave or convex lens, glass can magnify, intensify, and diminish inner and outer forms, images, and colors. The way in which light travels through glass and the possibility of changing its trajectory by cutting into its surface allow for dramatic visual effects. As is the case with gemstones, the more facets, the greater the brilliance from refracted light; the effects are most dramatic when the glass is completely transparent. As artist Gary Beechum commented, "I use the vessel as a sculptural form; the interior serves to contain light, color, and reflections rather than fruit or fluid."[2]

Current writers on studio glass, including Karen Chambers, Joan Falconer Byrd, Dan Klein, and Matthew Kangas, have discussed how the glass aesthetic reflects the artistic and cultural trends of the late twentieth century.[3] However, much of the literature addresses the history of the movement itself, glassmaking techniques, and the development of an individual artist's work, without touching on its relationship to the larger context of fine art in general.

To some extent, this is understandable, given that the movement is only thirty-six years old, and the early years were primarily devoted to learning and developing new techniques.[4] Nevertheless, while the Littleton-Labino discoveries allowed individual artists to experiment freely with new and original ways to express themselves in glass, they were not working in a vacuum. With the exception of some of the Europeans who received their training in trade schools or glass factories, the majority of the fifty-seven artists represented in this collection have university degrees, many in fine arts, and a number have been or currently are university professors. Littleton established the first course in glassblowing at the University of Wisconsin–Madison in 1964. By the mid-1970s more than one hundred university glass programs had been established in the United States alone.[5]

An analysis of many of the glass objects in the Aviva and Jack A. Robinson Studio Glass Collection provides a significant and diverse basis for arguing that glass, no less than other art media, is being employed to create fine art. This can be seen clearly when looking at these pieces in the context of the pluralism of late modern art.

The cultural concerns and historical events of the 1960s through the 1990s affected artists. The manufacturing society was developing into an information society. There was a growing concern about the environment, homelessness, AIDS, terrorism, and violence, as well as issues of ethnic, racial, national, religious, and sexual identity. Artists of this period have viewed their work as a weapon in the struggle to maintain their compassion in the midst of the world's increasing inhumanity. They have sought new ways of portraying political, economic, and social reality. This period can be characterized by the coexistence of diverse approaches to art, from abstraction to various forms of representation. Any technique, size, style, or medium could now be used as an expressive means, no matter how odd or unorthodox it might appear to some.

The style most prevalent in the 1960s when the first studio glass pieces were created was abstraction. Abstract and representational art are at the opposite ends of a continuum. Purely abstract art does not have recognizable subjects; representational art does. An abstract image can be grounded in an actual object; for example, in *Self Portrait II* (fig. 1), Joan Miró has formed long-lashed eyes into sunbursts or sharp-petaled daisies floating on a black background. Abstract art can also give visual form to something inherently nonvisual, such as emotions, sensations, or ideas. A work's meaning is intended to be grasped intuitively by the viewer.

An example of abstract art based on recognizable forms is *White Vessel Form* (no. 48), by Joel Philip Myers. On the surface, Myers has arranged abstracted shapes of clouds and mountains into ambiguous compositions. Myers was the first studio glass artist to negate one of the principal characteristics of glass: its transparency. He feels that in the past, the sheer attractiveness of the material often blinded the viewer to the meaning of his art. He thus works with an opaque matte surface that becomes a canvas for his two-dimensional arrangements. Myers's sophisticated use of drawing, pattern, and shape relationships can be traced to his earlier experiences in advertising and ceramics.

Other examples in the Robinson collection give visual form to something inherently nonvisual. After a successful six-year career as a graphic artist, Richard Ritter began to work in the three-dimensional medium of glass. Rather than abstracting real objects, in *YC-7-1984* (no. 65), Ritter seeks to evoke the sensation of an imaginary fluid world by suspending colored linear forms—derived from his graphic work—in clear glass. However, in contrast to a two-dimensional object, the interior space of *YC-7-1984* is penetrated by light, giving it a radiant luminosity. In addition, the thick glass acts like a lens, distorting the internal shapes and drawing the viewer into a seemingly infinite universe of subtle colorations and textures.

The abstract composition of shapes that appear to float in space in *Image Vessel #15072* (no. 1) is used by Herb Babcock to give form to a metaphor. He explained, "The metaphor was an extension of the triadic element based upon the trinity, the trilogy, and oriental concepts of spirit, reality and source, and other personal insights concerning the concept of three that I had been using in steel-fabrication sculpture."[6] As the eye scans *Image Vessel #15072*, color drifts in and out of focus from one side to another. Change the level of view, and the image changes. Change light direction or intensity, and the image responds.

A number of artists use color as their primary vehicle in creating abstract art. Called color field abstractions, the works are non-

FIGURE **1**
JOAN MIRÓ
Spanish, 1893–1983
Self Portrait II, 1938
Oil on burlap, 129.5 x 195.6 cm (51 x 77 in.)
Gift of W. Hawkins Ferry; 66.66.
© 1998 Artists Rights Society (ARS), New York/ADAGP, Paris

FIGURE **2**
PAUL JENKINS
American, born 1923
Phenomena Yield Blue Milk,
1964
Oil on canvas, 127 x 76.2 cm
(50 x 30 in.)
Founders Society Purchase,
Director's Discretionary Fund;
64.104. © Paul Jenkins

representational, and color is used to trigger emotional reactions. Color-field painters rejected illusions of depth in an attempt to eliminate any distinction between a subject and its background. For example, Paul Jenkins used diluted pigments to stain an untreated canvas in *Phenomena Yield Blue Milk* (fig. 2), producing an effect of thin veils floating back and forth across the surface.

Similarly, Dominick Labino created a veiling effect in *Untitled* (no. 31) from his Emergence series. Labino, who held sixty patents for inventions, had a highly successful career as a scientist and engineer. In 1965 he retired and set up his own glass-making establishment, where he experimented with the chemistry of color. Whether or not Labino was consciously practicing color field theories, as Karen Chambers has said, "his 'Emergence' series is the glass-world equivalent of the color-field school of paintings."[7]

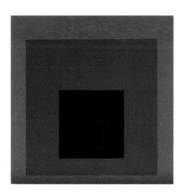

FIGURE **3**
JOSEF ALBERS
American, 1888–1976
Homage to the Square, 1964
Oil on panel, 61 x 61 cm
(24 x 24 in.)
Gift of Anni Albers and
The Josef Albers Foundation;
79.172. © 1998 Albers Foundation/
Artists Rights Society (ARS),
New York

Harvey Littleton created *Cardioid Sectioned* (no. 36) as part of a series in which he experimented with color. These recall such studies as *Homage to the Square* (fig. 3) by Josef Albers who, during the 1950s and 1960s, explored the changing relationships of solid-colored squares within other fields of color. In *Cardioid Sectioned*, Littleton encased concentric bands of colored glass in crystal so that they appear to be floating. He then sliced the cylinder so light reflects off the edges and concentrates in the curves.

The work of Gary Beechum demonstrates an interest in the abstract use of color derived, to some extent, from his work as a studio assistant to Littleton in North Carolina from 1980 to 1988. As the title implies, in *Double Textile Vessel* (no. 3) Beechum is interested in fabric patterns. He wove rods of colored glass into intricate designs, which he then engulfed in a thick wall of clear glass.

Color and pattern also fascinate Klaus Moje. He had no formal art training but began as a glass cutter and polisher. Originally from Germany, he moved in 1982 to Australia, where he was greatly influenced by the spectacular sunsets, intensity of light, and dramatic landforms. The abstract work *Untitled* (no. 43), from his Shield series, is a pointed oval shape divided into sections. The area of intense stripes of orange, pink, black, and white evokes the shimmering air of Australia. At the opposite end, these same colors appear in a bold, rickrack pattern reminiscent of Aboriginal art. Geoffrey Edwards observed that Moje's works embody the same aesthetic purpose that underlies the stripe-and-lozenge canvases of color-field painter Kenneth Noland (see fig. 4).[8]

FIGURE **4**
KENNETH NOLAND
American, born 1924
Purple in the Shadow of Red, 1963
Acrylic on canvas, 182.9 x 182.9 cm (72 x 72 in.)
Founders Society Purchase, Dr. and Mrs. George Kamperman Fund; 64.100. © Kenneth Noland/Licensed by VAGA, New York, N.Y.

Toots Zynsky likens her glassmaking process to painting, because in both she creates an image or form by building up layers, either of paint or of colored glass threads. She draws on her visions and moods in creating abstract works and determining the colors. *Silk Bowl* (no. 78) was inspired by a dream she had about Africa prior to a six-month sojourn in Ghana. The colors express her emotions and ideas about the exuberant shades juxtaposed in African textiles, and the alternating color stripes suggest the rhythm of African dance. This bowl-shaped vessel is made of fused threads of Venetian glass that create a three-dimensional color-field painting.

Optical art, or Op Art, is a form of abstraction that creates the illusion of movement or three-dimensionality through the use of line, form, pattern, or color. An example is *Convexity* (fig. 5), a painting by Richard Anuskiewicz. The effects are produced as the viewer moves in front of the work. The viewer is not a passive or merely receptive observer of *Convexity*, but rather an active partner, interacting with the piece in order to animate it.

Sydney Cash has had no formal training in glassmaking; his education is in mathematics, the principles of which he has employed to create sculptures. He was clearly influenced by Op Art. Yet while Op Art is an art of surfaces, Cash's is one of layers of depth. *Ophthalmologic Intention* (no. 10) contains a wall of

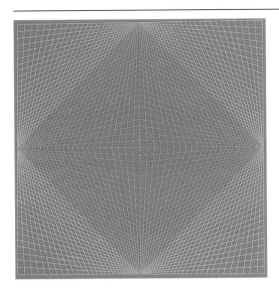

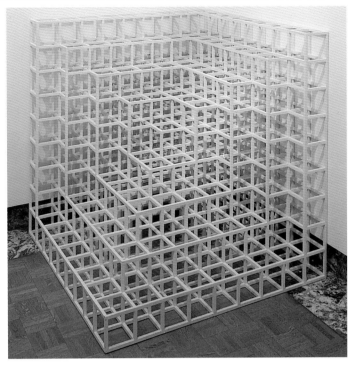

patterned glass that divides the space, distorting the moiré pattern of lines on the back wall while acting as a backdrop for the fragile wire structure over which molten glass sags as if frozen in motion. This work was inspired by Cash's intense curiosity about the dichotomy between the physical and the metaphysical, the material and the spiritual. To explore these concepts, he engages the observer's perception of movement, both real—the more the viewer changes perspective, the more the shifting plane of patterns creates ambiguous spaces that resist focus—and illusionary, in the suggested effect of gravitation on melting glass.

Without a doubt, some of the most alluring glass sculptures are those abstract forms that explore the many possibilities afforded by the behavior of glass in light. For *#85102* (no. 41) Paul Manners used glass cut into geometric forms with sharp angles that he glued together to create a sculpture. As light penetrates, passes through, and bounces off the acute angles and faceted edges, it transforms the work into a dynamic rainbow of colliding colors, clashing reflections, and intricate visual patterns. Manners hopes these works will "dissolve our visible world and allow us to become lost and transformed in various levels of reality."9

The dazzling visual effects created as light refracts through geometric forms when the sculpture is seen from different angles is what first draws the viewer to Jon Kuhn's work. Yet it is only after overcoming the appeal of the brilliant showers of changing color that a deeper engagement can occur, revealing what lies beneath the surface. The metaphor at the heart of Kuhn's work derives from his study of Eastern philosophy: in the figurative sense, this is the perfection within. In *Fleeting Umber* (no. 30) Kuhn represents this as a cube or "jewel" that appears

to float in the center of the glass structure. Kuhn said, "My work is not about beauty in itself. What is more beautiful than spirituality, the light within each of us?"10

Just as some abstract artists use color, optical effects, or light to create forms that do not represent observable objects, others use space. Under most conditions, space is relatively invisible: it is only perceived by its boundaries.

Ginny Ruffner makes abstract sculptural containers. *Parallel Universe/Overcast* (no. 66) from the Dancing Box series is a colorful glass grid that outlines an interior space with openings that allow for an interaction with exterior space. Artists such as Ruffner and Sol LeWitt—in works such as *Modular Open Cube Pieces* (fig. 6)—have rejected the traditional idea of a sculpture as an isolated object displayed on a pedestal, made of marble or bronze, and surrounded by space. Instead, they conceive of sculpture as three-dimensional environments that define space. However, while LeWitt's clean white cubes were industrially fabricated from plans based on mathematical systems, Ruffner's merry, organic shapes were hand formed and colored.

The French artist Etienne Leperlier is also interested in the manifestation of the abstract concept of space. *Anatomie d'Ombre II* (no. 32) belongs to a series of works based on "L'Ombre, l'Empreinte, et le Reflet" (Shadow, Imprint, and Reflection), a personal trilogy that represents the three possible manifestations of reality. "This piece illustrates l'Ombre = shadow: it refers to the shadow cone which appears when there is a solar eclipse. I materialized this shadow cone in order to be able to imagine what could be hiding inside, and then I dissected it and I represented what I could see inside."[11] The translucency of the *pâte de verre* glass and the opulence of the blue glass in the interior are emphasized as light streams through the openings in the sculpture.

By the 1970s the dominance of abstract art was being challenged by representational art. Representational art refers to works with a recognizable subject. Several examples in the Robinson collection reveal this renewed interest in some of the more traditional subjects and themes of representational art: the figure, nature, architecture, and the urban environment.

In the late twentieth century, the human figure has been used to explore issues of personal identity. This is an art of self-consciousness—literally, consciousness of the self—which artists capture in their portrayal of humans, their emotions, and psychic states. For instance, in the painting *Glance* (fig. 7) by R. B. Kitaj, the private moment shared between the man and woman as they glance at one another is suggestive and potent. Yet despite their interaction, the characters—one of whom likely represents Kitaj himself—are isolated from one another, separated physically by the powerful diagonal of the bench and emotionally by their expressions and body language.

FIGURE **7**
R. B. KITAJ
American, born 1932
Glance, 1992
Oil on canvas, 121.9 x 121.9 cm (48 x 48 in.)
Founders Society Purchase, W. Hawkins Ferry Fund; 1995.49.
© R.B. Kitaj, courtesy, Marlborough Gallery

FIGURE **8**
JOSEPH CORNELL
American, 1903–72
Night Songs, 1953–55
Mixed media, height 26 cm (10¼ in.)
Founders Society Purchase, W. Hawkins Ferry Fund, Catherine Kresge Dewey Fund, Gift of Mrs. George Kamperman, by exchange; 1993.77. © The Joseph and Robert Cornell Memorial Foundation

Stephen Hodder confronts his own identity in *Regaining the Edge* (no. 24). The expressionistic forms and colors, combined with personal symbols, deny the viewer any certainty about their meaning. Hodder explains, "This particular work was about personally reestablishing clarity following a long period of confusion. Over the years I had developed a way of working with symbols and images that came from the far reaches of my own memory and consciousness and was applying it to every situation in my life as a means to learn more about myself and those around me. Basically I am motivated to search my own soul and psyche for the residue of experiences universal to the human condition."[12]

Another self portrait is *Bird Storm* (no. 70) by Therman Statom. Like Joseph Cornell in *Night Songs* (fig. 8), Statom adopts the technique of assemblage, in which non-art objects and materials, including found objects and even junk, are transformed into sculpture. Both artists use shallow glass boxes to enclose portraits. In *Night Songs*, a reproduction of a sixteenth-century painting of an anonymous youth, somber in demeanor, is placed behind blue glass. Through his choice and arrangement of objects, Cornell has created a personal world that only he understands. Equally puzzling is Statom's personal mythology. The glass surfaces are painted with broad, colorful brushstrokes. The boxes are filled with vignettes of found objects that suggest an intriguing, but ambiguous, narrative content.

As the title suggests, *The Engineer, or My Father as a Young Man* (no. 61) is a portrait of Clifford Rainey's father. The figure's body has been sliced, with plates of glass inserted between the layers. A metal support is impressed with the outlines of tools that refer to the father's profession. The fragmentation of this sculpture portrays a condition we identify with contemporary humanity—never whole but constantly faced with conflict, danger, and insecurity.

Two Guys (no. 25) by David Hopper was inspired by America's awakening to the AIDS epidemic.[13] The high-pitched emotional content of this sculpture depicting suffering human beings illustrates the horrors of the disease. By encasing these two figures in solid molten glass, Hopper depicts metaphorically the invisible barrier that society has created around AIDS victims. They are imprisoned, preserved, and protected like biological specimens.

Terrorism and violence are certainly not new to the world, but beginning in the 1980s they have escalated worldwide. *The Beast* (no. 77) by Czesław Zuber represents this cruel, evil side of humanity. Created from a massive piece of glass that he broke with a hammer, the grotesque head with sharp, jagged edges suggests the threat of injury. Zuber used luminous neon colors to outline the gaping mouth, outstretched tongue, and enormous eyes. For Zuber, the head is the symbol for the seat of the mind; the mouth, which swallows the nourishment necessary for life, both cries out in pain and shows teeth in a sign of aggression; and the eyes symbolize the mind's apprehension of reality.[14]

Thomas Scoon suggests another, more positive aspect of humanity. In *Blue Hill Boy #3* (no. 68) the fragility of the cast glass is juxtaposed with the massive presence of granite and sandstone (from the Blue Hills Indian Reservation in Milton, Massachusetts) to suggest a human form. Humans have always related their form with the earth: metaphorically we refer to "mother earth," and physically, at death, our bodies return to the earth. In *Blue Hill Boy #3*, Scoon symbolically depicts this relationship by creating the figure from rough, jagged rocks and cast glass; the earth and its geological foundations become equivalents of human physicality.

In *Slave* (no. 39) Mária Lugossy depicts a human body made of bronze enclosed in layers of earth depicted in glass. She is interested in two opposing aspects of nature—the hardness of rock formations and the softness of organic form. Tension results from the hopelessness of trying to break out. Lugossy describes her work: "Our existence can be traced back to the moment when the Primeval Sea had finally born us to the full time. We drifted along with the currents of aeons and, sinking into a deep sleep for millions of years, we went on hiding in the creases of

FIGURE **9**
DONALD SULTAN
American, born 1951
Oranges on a Branch March 14, 1922, 1992
Tar, spackle, and oil on tiles over masonite, 2.4 x 2.4 m
(96 x 96 in.)
Founders Society Purchase, Catherine Kresge Dewey
Fund, and W. Hawkins Ferry Fund; 1994.19.
Reproduced courtesy of the artist

geological strata. Those incapable of living turned into inclusions in rocks—fossils now, they can be found even today."[15]

Nature, both romanticized and threatened, has inspired artists in the late twentieth century. Mark Peiser adopted the romantic view in his landscape vase *Live Oaks and Spanish Moss* (no. 55). It was influenced by his long walks in the woods, where he experienced an inner peace that he captures in this idyll of quiet beauty. This vessel functions in the round as a seamlessly constructed visual whole that the viewer can imagine entering. Equally romantic is the Czech artist Pavel Hlava. In *Arise* (no. 23) Hlava generalized the natural form of a brilliant sunrise and its prismatic colors in a simple, unfolding fanlike shape.

Image Valley (no. 28) by Kreg Kallenberger was influenced by his experience of such dramatic environments as the ice-encrusted mountains of Greenland and the red rock towers of Sedona, Arizona.[16] As in Op Art, the illusionary landscape of *Image Valley* appears and disappears, becomes enlarged, reduced, and distorted as the viewer circles the sculpture. Kallenberger achieves this effect by combining glass, oil staining, and stone. The opacity of the soft pastel stains that evoke the red clay, burned grass, and scrub oak of Arizona is in dramatic contrast to the brilliance of the painstakingly polished glass form.

In the 1980s, nature gained a heightened respectability as subject matter as artists reacted to industrial disasters and the exploitation of the earth's resources. For instance, in *Oranges on a Branch March 14, 1992* (fig. 9) Donald Sultan exploits the eroticism of the plump, ripe fruit, depicted against a black surface made of tar, calling to mind the vulnerability of plants and animals to oil spills.

Ulrica Hydman-Vallien is a painter who uses glass vessels as a canvas to depict her dreamlike fantasies. The meaning of the narrative implied in the title *Running Around Forever* (no. 27) is as ambiguous as that of Statom's *Bird Storm*. However, because the large, playful hybrid animals appear to be transporting the small humans through an area filled with boulders, the relationship may have to do with the threat humans pose to animals and nature.

In *Cadmium Red Light Venetian* (no. 14) Dale Chihuly has used shapes and colors found in nature as his point of departure to create a huge, vividly hued, stylized organic shape which seems to represent an outlandish tropical flower. The title is suggestive: cadmium red is a common artists' pigment that varies in intensity from light red to maroon; a red light is a warning signal but also brings to mind a red-light district, perhaps in Venice. This play of words, as well as the riotous color and the overpowering organic force of *Cadmium Red Light Venetian* was observed by Mary Douglas: "[Chihuly's] 'Venetian' series . . . present a caricature of decorative arts that incorporates references to gargantuan table lamps, '60s glass vases, 19th century satin glass, and the interior decor of discotheques and bachelor pads . . . The garish palette and the flamboyant, excessive forms imply camp; the 'Venetians' are the Divines, the drag queens, of glass art . . . This flower erotica is a cross between Robert Mapplethorpe's *Calla Lily* [see fig. 10] and Louis Comfort Tiffany's *Jack-in-the-Pulpit Vase* [fig. 11]."[17]

Figure **11**
LOUIS COMFORT TIFFANY
American, 1848–1933
Jack-in-the-Pulpit Vase, 1915
Glass, height 49.53 cm (19½ in.)
Founders Society Purchase, American Art General Fund, and funds from Jerome M. and Patricia J. Shaw; 1990.295

Architecture and the urban environment constitute another area of renewed interest for artists. *Golden Chapel* (no. 5) by Zoltán Bohus brings to mind a cathedral. He achieves this not because the piece looks like a religious edifice, but because it evokes the essence of religious architecture, with its passage from exterior to interior, from secular to sacred. Light, often a symbol of spirituality, passes through the work and is diffused into a soft glow, suggesting infinity.

Images of environmental pollution and urban decay are represented in the disquieting art of Jay Musler. The edges of *The Architectural Bowl* (no. 46) have been cut and broken to express the sinister nature of the contemporary urban landscape; the beauty of the glass is shrouded behind a veil of gray paint reminiscent of the smoke and grime of cities.

Two columnlike works in the Robinson collection are references to architecture, but unlike true columns, these do not support a structure. Rather, they are about the idea of columns. A soft shimmer of light appears to illuminate Howard Ben Tré's *Structure #5* (no. 4) from within: as the copper inside the sculpture oxidizes with the passing of time, it acquires a green patina very much in sympathy with the tint of the glass. The light that glows green as it passes through the jagged-edged glass plates of *Stonelith #102* (no. 60) by Damian Priour makes the

Figure **10**
ROBERT MAPPLETHORPE
American, 1946–89
Calla Lily, 1988
Lithograph printed in black ink on wove paper,
sheet: 65.7 x 64.4 cm (24⅞ x 25½ in.)
Founders Society Purchase, Benson and Edith Ford Fund and funds generated by the Detroit Institute of Arts Photography Department; 1993.67.1–2. Copyright © the Estate of Robert Mapplethorpe, used by permission

FIGURE **12**
KIKI SMITH
American, born 1954
Lot's Wife, 1996
Bronze and silica with steel stand,
205.7 x 68.6 x 66 cm
(81 x 27 x 26 in.)
Founders Society Purchase,
W. Hawkins Ferry Fund, with
funds from the Friends of Modern
Art; 1997.43. Reproduced courtesy
of the artist

is composed of twelve pieces, five of which are molded heads of sand-blasted glass; the others combine to depict portions of the macabre, expressionistic, fragmented face of Osiris encased within glass. In contemporary terms, the myth of Osiris represents today's individual search, often through psychotherapy, to uncover the influences or events that cause unease and to reunify these parts in a way that brings satisfaction.

The little-understood areas of human pre-history hold a special fascination for William Morris. *Suspended Artifact* (no. 44) appropriates primeval images such as those found deep inside Chauvet Cave in the Ardèche Valley of southeastern France; they were discovered in 1994, the same year that Morris created this sculpture, although there may be no direct connection. Morris's sculpture is an astonishing rendering in blown glass of a piece of baleen or whale bone and an animal skin suspended from a spear. A leaping deer with large antlers is drawn on the animal skin in the manner of an ancient cave painting. Spear, whale bone, and animal skin all refer to a hunting society and the elemental struggle between humans and nature. By making them of glass, Morris symbolizes the transitory, fragile quality of life.

With the increasing permissiveness of late modern art came a blurring of the boundaries that had traditionally separated craft and art. This set the stage for the acceptance of artists' furniture as a hybrid art form. Examples of furniture by artists such as Pablo Picasso and Constantin Brancusi date back as far as the early twentieth century. However, unlike later artists who created furniture, they were not interested in conveying meaning through these works, but in creating unique, functional forms.[18]

Although *Chair #1* (no. 16) is functional, artist Maxwell Davis is more interested in the meaning it conveys than in its usability. Davis challenges the sitter to consider just what a chair is by constructing the seat and back of broken glass. The blown glass legs represent the organic, sensuous nature of glass, and the broken, machine-made sheet glass represents the medium's cold, hard, and threatening nature. Davis said that he sees broken glass daily in Detroit; it carries the connotation of danger, and he "wanted to create a situation where broken glass is both functional and non-threatening when in contact with a person. I was also interested in the idea of recycling—using something viewed as not having value (broken glass) and making it valuable."[19]

José Chardiet is inspired by everyday objects: tables, chairs, knives, cups, bowls. *Zebra Mesa* (no. 11) is a table (*mesa* in Spanish) with indentations holding two vertical spiky objects and a bowl, all decorated in dark stripes. The surface, with its ambiguous objects, suggests a place of sacrifice or worship, a place where a mysterious rite could be performed. The reference to an animal, the roughness of the forms and their surfaces,

limestone appear to float in the air. The two sculptures are illusions and allusions. They refer to ancient monuments and vanished cities, civilizations beginning and ending, falling down and being rebuilt. The sculptures deal with issues of permanence and fragility, destruction and renewal, and the effects of humans on the natural world. Ben Tré and Priour both emphasize the passing of time: the oxidizing copper of *Structure #5* and the limestone, imprinted with ancient fossils, of *Stonelith #102*.

Some late modern art makes reference to and transforms already existing art in ways that make a fresh statement. Instead of striving for originality, many artists recently have concentrated on the way images and symbols shift or lose their meaning when put into different contexts. They borrow ideas and forms from the past and use them in a new way. For example, the life-size, silica bronze sculpture *Lot's Wife* (fig. 12) by Kiki Smith takes its subject from the biblical story of the destruction of Sodom and Gomorrah. But Smith's interpretation of this story is nontraditional: the anonymity of Lot's wife and her harsh punishment for her sanction of—or at least curiosity about—sexual permissiveness suggest to Smith parallels with contemporary mores.

Another borrowed story is told by Kenneth Carder's *Osiris* (no. 8). Osiris, the ancient Egyptian god of the afterlife, was slain by his evil brother Seth and torn into pieces. Upon learning of this, Isis, the wife of Osiris, journeyed forth in search of her husband's remains. Wherever Isis found a portion of the corpse, she buried it and built a shrine to mark the spot. Carder's sculpture and the uncertainty of what the objects and bowl are to be used for recall the enigmatic rituals performed by early humans.

The Robinson collection is a rich assemblage of works that vividly reflect life and art in the contemporary world. The objects in this collection demonstrate that the development of the studio glass movement over the past thirty-six years is founded on the same aesthetic conceptions as the traditional fine art media. In the past, art historians have taught the history of late-twentieth-century art primarily by using examples of painting, sculpture, and architecture. Given the varied aesthetic approaches of many other media—traditionally relegated to the status of "crafts"—as seen here in the Robinson collection of studio glass, this exclusivity is no longer necessary or appropriate.

NOTES

1 I wish to thank MaryAnn Wilkinson, curator of Twentieth-Century Art at the DIA, for posing these questions.

2 Artist's statement, DIA curatorial files, July 26, 1983.

3 See Klein 1989, 8–16; Byrd 1989; Kangas 1997a; Kangas 1997b; Chambers 1995; Chambers 1996.

4 For a detailed history of the studio glass movement, see Frantz 1989 and Klein 1989.

5 Klein 1989, 8.

6 Artist's statement, DIA curatorial files, 1981.

7 Chambers 1997, 33.

8 Edwards 1995, 13.

9 Artist's statement, DIA curatorial files, undated.

10 Boca Raton 1996, 9.

11 Letter to the author, DIA curatorial files, April 26, 1996.

12 Letter to the author, DIA curatorial files, February 22, 1996.

13 Letter to the author, DIA curatorial files, February 20, 1996.

14 Paris 1989, 8.

15 Ricke 1990, 44.

16 Artist's statement, DIA curatorial files, undated.

17 Douglas 1992, 6.

18 For early attempts to introduce seating furniture made of glass to the market, see Smith 1991, 77, and Saint Louis 1995, 153.

19 Letter to the author, DIA curatorial files, March 4, 1996.

Catalogue

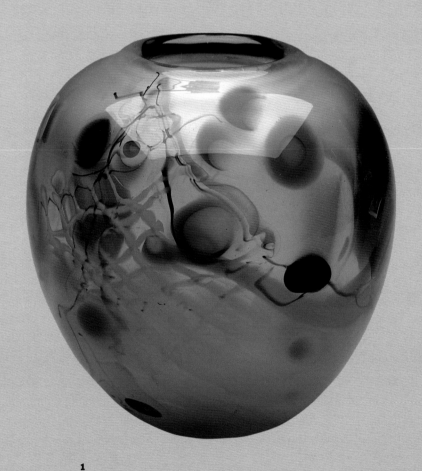

1

HERB BABCOCK

Image Vessel #15072
1978
Blown glass
Height 11.4 cm (4½ in.)
1996.147

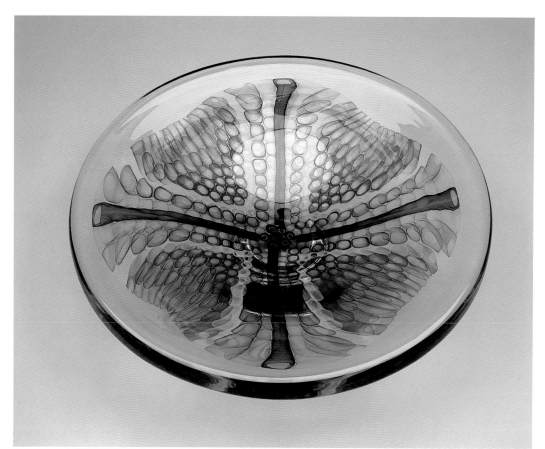

GARY BEECHUM

Color Study Vessel
1983
Blown glass
Height 7.6 cm (3 in.)
1996.139

24

3

GARY BEECHUM

Double Textile Vessel
1983
Blown glass
Height 20.3 cm (8 in.)
1996.124

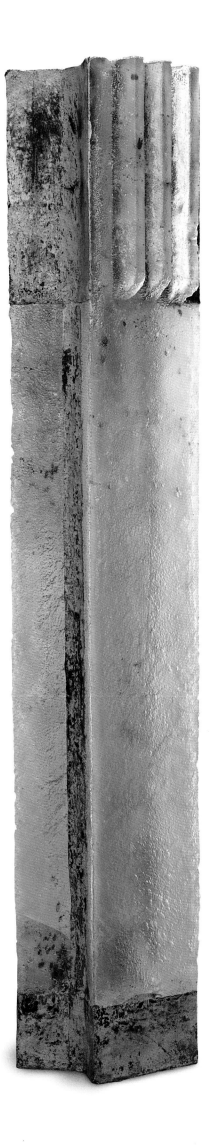

4

HOWARD BEN TRÉ

Structure #5
1983
Cast glass, copper
Height 104.1 cm (41 in.)
1996.91

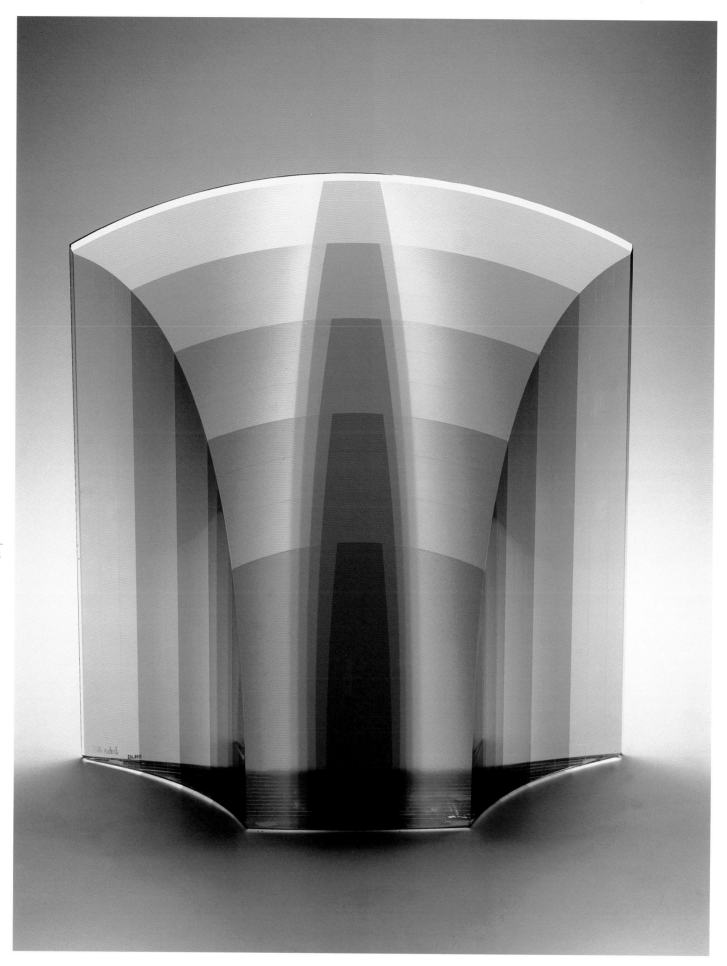

5

ZOLTÁN BOHUS

Golden Chapel
1995
Plate glass
Height 38.1 cm (15 in.)
1996.113

6

CURTISS R. BROCK

Stone Vessel
1984
Blown glass
Height 35.6 cm (14 in.)
1996.153

7

JANE BRUCE

Large Plate
1988
Blown glass
Height 12.7 cm (5 in.)
1996.137

8
KENNETH CARDER

Osiris
1985
Blown glass
Height 35.6 cm (14 in.)
1996.109

9

WILLIAM CARLSON

Compression Series
1980
Cast and Vitrolite glass
Height 30.5 cm (12 in.)
1996.156

10
SYDNEY CASH

Ophthalmologic Intention
1988
Plate and pattern glass, wire
Height 27.9 cm (11 in.)
1996.133

11

JOSÉ CHARDIET

Zebra Mesa
1987
Cast glass
Height 101.6 cm (40 in.)
1996.86

12

JOSÉ CHARDIET

Head #2
1994
Blown glass
Height 99.1 cm (39 in.)
1996.87

13

DALE CHIHULY

Korallrot Basket Series
1977
Blown glass
Height 33 cm (13 in.)
1996.92

14

DALE CHIHULY

Cadmium Red Light Venetian
1989
Blown glass
Height 35.6 cm (14 in.)
1996.116

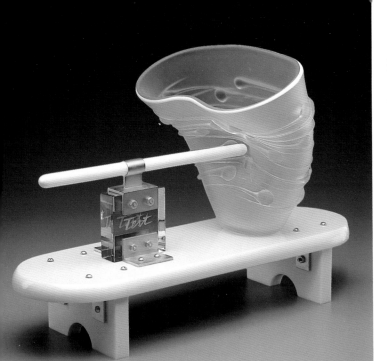

15

DAN DAILEY

Test from the Distorted Vessels
series
1981
Plate, blown, and Vitrolite glass
Height 30.5 cm (12 in.)
1996.131

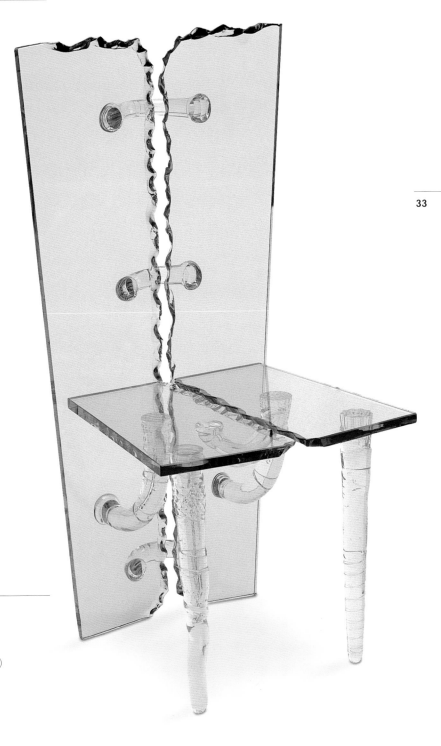

16

MAXWELL DAVIS

Chair #1
1988
Blown and plate glass
Height 106.7 cm (42 in.)
1996.134

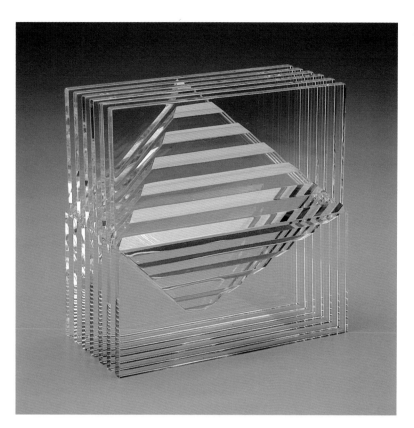

17

STEVEN DEVRIES

Double Tetrahedron SRDI
1984
Plate glass
Height 15.2 cm (6 in.)
1996.125

18

STEPHEN DEE EDWARDS

Lattice Physalia and *Ocean Dancer*
1983
Blown glass
Height A. 38 cm (15 in.)
Height B. 27.9 cm (11 in.)
1996.160

19

BOHUMIL ELIÁŠ

Penetration
1993
Plate glass
Height 55.9 cm (22 in.)
1996.98

20

MICHAEL GLANCY

Ruby Gold Synthesis
1988
Blown and plate glass
Height 20.3 cm (8 in.)
1996.112

21
PAVEL HLAVA

Cosmos Cycle
1982
Blown glass
Height 27.9 cm (11 in.)
1996.130

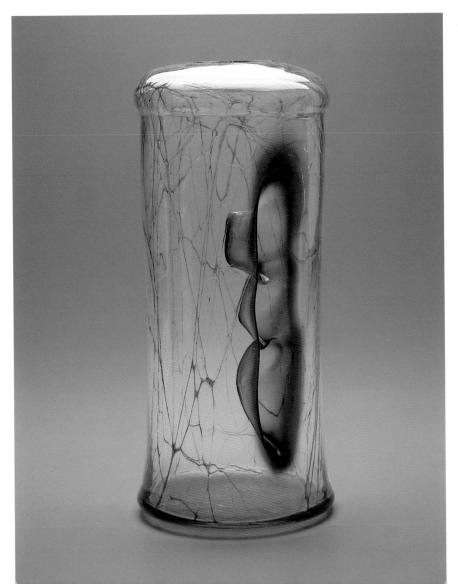

22
PAVEL HLAVA

Nature Cycle
1982
Blown glass
Height 35.6 cm (14 in.)
1996.158

23

PAVEL HLAVA

Arise
1994
Cast glass
Height 43.2 cm (17 in.)
1996.120

24

W. STEPHEN HODDER

Regaining the Edge
1990
Blown glass
Height 48.3 cm (19 in.)
1996.121

25

DAVID HOPPER

Two Guys
1988
Blown glass
Height 35.6 cm (14 in.)
1996.135

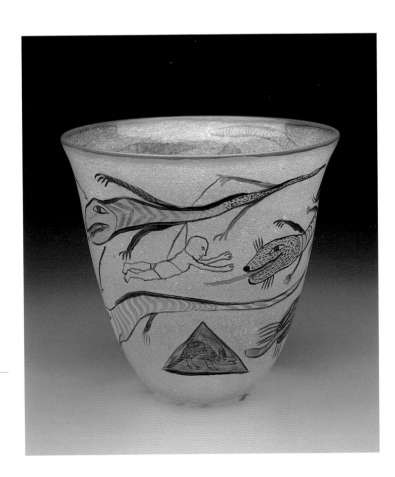

27

ULRICA HYDMAN-VALLIEN

Running Around Forever
1978
Blown glass
Height 22.9 cm (9 in.)
1996.106

28

KREG KALLENBERGER

Image Valley
1995
Cast glass, stone
Height 34.3 cm (13½ in.)
1996.114

29

JON KUHN

Vase
1979
Blown glass
Height 33 cm (13 in.)
1996.154

30

JON KUHN

Fleeting Umber
1992
Fabricated glass
Height 20.3 cm (8 in.)
1996.115

31

DOMINICK LABINO

Untitled from the Emergence series
1974
Blown glass
Height 21.6 cm (8½ in.)
1996.110

ETIENNE LEPERLIER

Anatomie d'Ombre II
1993
Cast glass
Height 62.2 cm (24½ in.)
1996.118

33

MARVIN LIPOFSKY

Split Piece from the Venini series
1975
Blown glass
Blown at the Venini Factory,
Murano, Italy, with help from
Maestro Gianni Toso
Height 17.8 cm (7 in.)
1996.123

34

MARVIN LIPOFSKY

*Serie Crystalex Hantich, Nóvy
Bor, Czechoslovakia #015*
1982
Blown glass
Blown at the Crystalex, Hantich
Factory, Nóvy Bor,
Czechoslovakia, with help from
Glassmaster Petr Novotny, assisted
by Carol Schreitmuller
Height 40.6 cm (16 in.)
1996.149

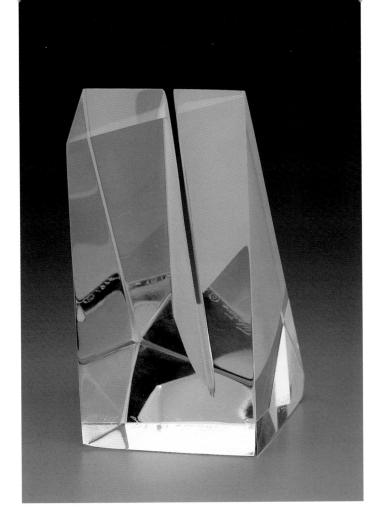

35

HARVEY K. LITTLETON

Untitled
1978
Blown glass
Height 11.4 cm (4½ in.)
1996.129

36

HARVEY K. LITTLETON

Cardioid Sectioned from the Solid
Geometry series
1980
Blown glass
Height 27.9 cm (11 in.)
1996.108

JOHN LUEBTOW

LF-24-86/12 from the Linear
Form series
1986
Plate glass
Height 38.1 cm (15 in.)
1996.159

38

MÁRIA LUGOSSY

Geomorphosis
1987
Plate glass
Height 31.8 cm (12½ in.)
1996.94

39

MÁRIA LUGOSSY

Slave
1994
Plate glass, bronze
Height 7.6 cm (3 in.)
1996.126

**FLORA C. MACE AND JOEY
KIRKPATRICK**

Figure Harp
1984
Blown glass, wire
Height 86.4 cm (34 in.)
1996.136

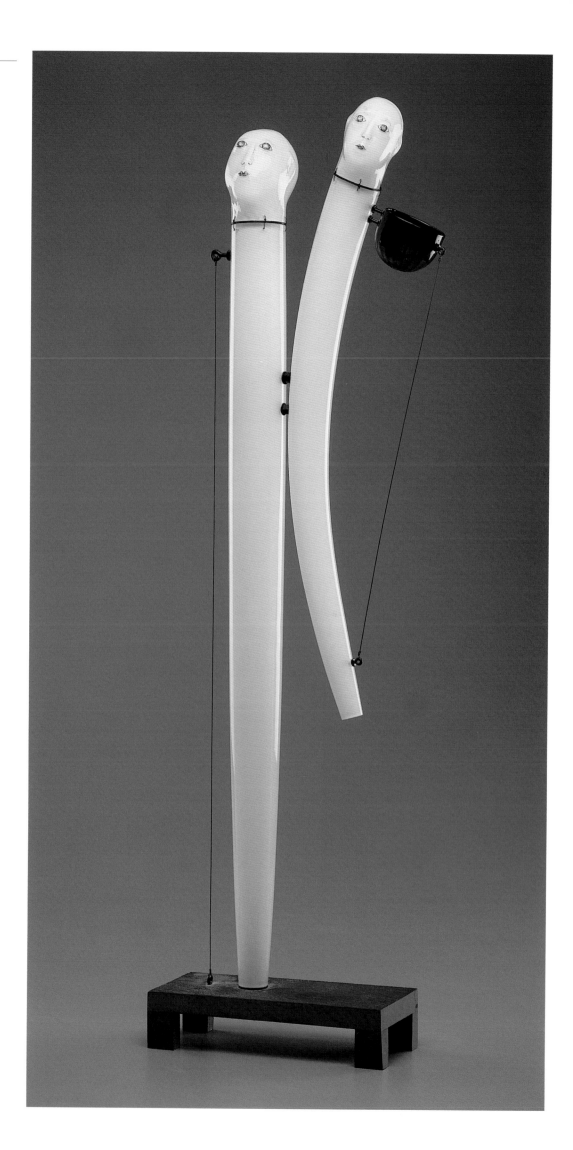

41

PAUL MANNERS

#85102
1985
Fabricated glass
Height 15.2 cm (6 in.)
1996.111

42

PAUL MANNERS

Pythias
1986
Fabricated glass
Height 15.2 cm (6 in.)
1996.96

43
KLAUS MOJE

Untitled from the Shield series
1985
Mosaic glass
Height 2.5 cm (1 in.)
1996.138

44

WILLIAM MORRIS

Suspended Artifact
1994
Blown glass
Height 88.9 cm (35 in.)
1996.99

45
SHINICHI MURO

Ship of King
1993
Blown glass
Height 25.4 cm (10 in.)
1996.107

46
JAY MUSLER

The Architectural Bowl
1981
Fabricated glass
Height 25.4 cm (10 in.)
1996.88

JOEL PHILIP MYERS

Untitled
1977
Blown glass
Height 16.5 cm (6½ in.)
1996.103

48

JOEL PHILIP MYERS

White Vessel Form from the
Contiguous Fragment series
1979
Blown glass
Height 17.8 cm (7 in.)
1996.102

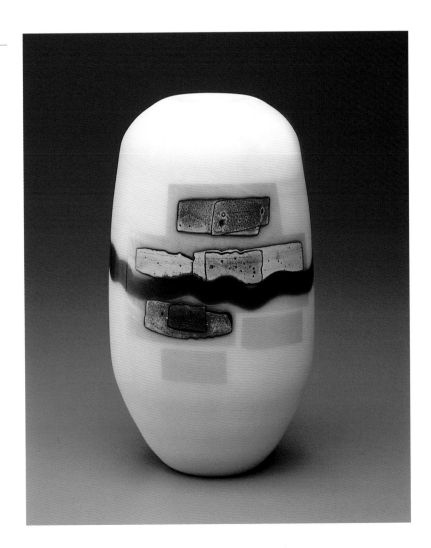

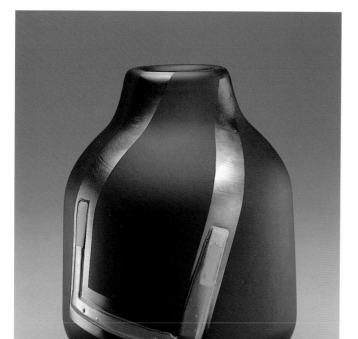

49

JOEL PHILIP MYERS

Black Vessel Form from the
Contiguous Fragment series
1979
Blown glass
Height 22.9 cm (9 in.)
1996.104

50

JOEL PHILIP MYERS

Vessel Form
1985
Blown glass
Height 33 cm (13 in.)
1996.105

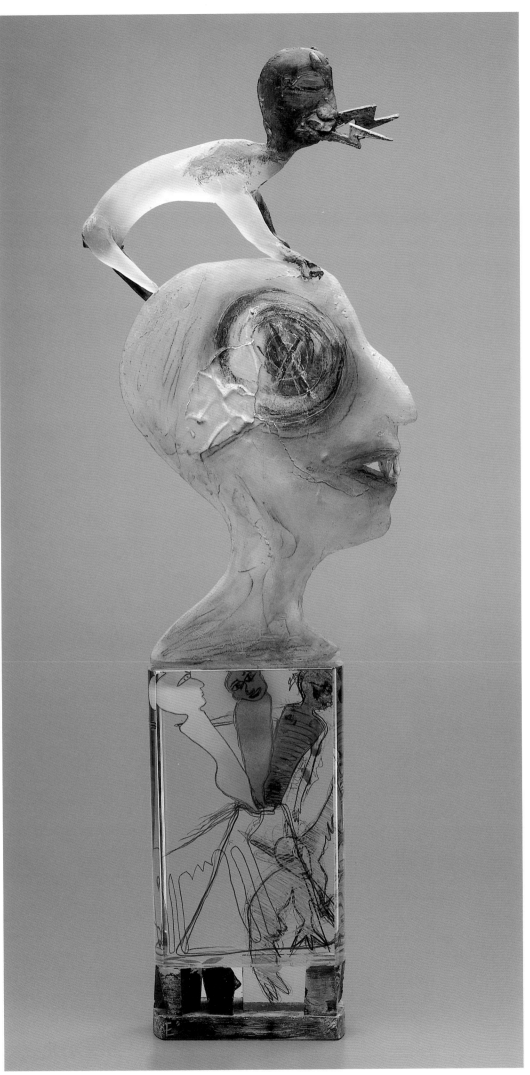

ROBERT PALUSKY

The Cost of Fame
1989
Cast glass
Height 73.7 cm (29 in.)
1996.150

52

MICHAEL PAVLIK

Cylinder Form
1978
Blown glass
Height 22.9 cm (9 in.)
1996.144

53

MICHAEL PAVLIK

Gate to Inner World
1995
Fabricated glass
Height 33 cm (13 in.)
1996.95

54

MARK PEISER

IS152 from the Inner Space series
1984
Fabricated glass
Height 22.9 cm (9 in.)
1996.128

59

55

MARK PEISER

Live Oaks and Spanish Moss
from the Paperweight Vase series
1978
Blown glass
Height 22.9 cm (9 in.)
1996.101

56

MARK PEISER

IS055 from the Inner Space series
1983
Fabricated glass
Height 19.1 cm (7½ in.)
1996.127

STEPHEN ROLFE POWELL

Michigan Hot Glass Workshop
Demo Piece
1995
Blown glass
Height 72.4 cm (28½ in.)
1996.117

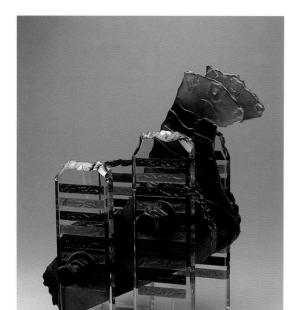

58

DAMIAN PRIOUR

Primitive Pet
1985
Plate glass, found objects
Height 35.6 cm (14 in.)
1996.152

59

DAMIAN PRIOUR

Columna Del Mar
1986
Plate glass
Height 190.5 cm (75 in.)
1996.89

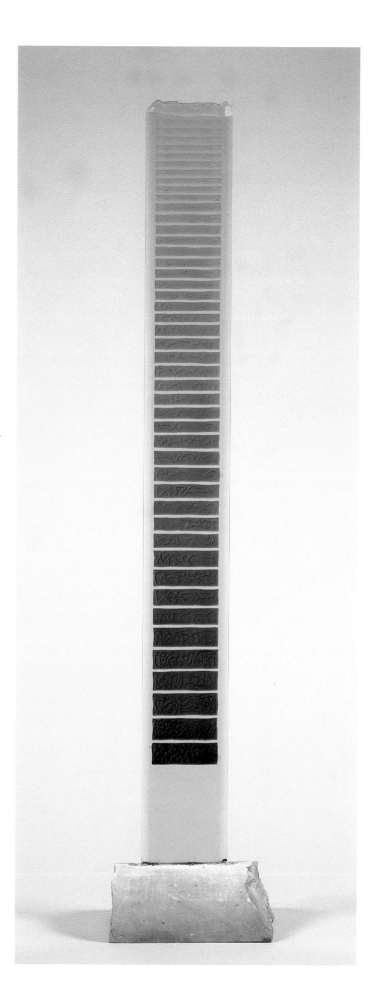

60
DAMIAN PRIOUR

Stonelith #102
1986
Plate glass, limestone
Height 181.6 cm (71½ in.)
1996.141

64

CLIFFORD RAINEY

*The Engineer, or My Father as a
Young Man* from the Chuland series
1986
Cast glass, metal
Height 58.4 cm (23 in.)
1996.90

62

RICHARD Q. RITTER, JR.

Untitled
1971
Blown glass
Height 25.4 cm (10 in.)
1996.145

63

RICHARD Q. RITTER, JR.

Untitled
1975–76
Blown glass
Height 12.7 cm (5 in.)
1996.143

RICHARD Q. RITTER, JR.

YC-29A-1982
1982
Blown glass
Height 17.8 cm (7 in.)
1996.132

65
RICHARD Q. RITTER, JR.

YC-7-1984
1984
Blown glass
Height 15.2 cm (6 in.)
1996.157

66
GINNY RUFFNER

Parallel Universe/Overcast from the Dancing Box series
1985
Lampworked glass
Height 61 cm (24 in.)
1996.146

KARL SCHANTZ

Urban Rainbow #7 from the
XJ19 series
1984
Vitrolite glass
Height 20.3 cm (8 in.)
1996.142

68

THOMAS SCOON

Blue Hill Boy #3
1989
Cast glass, granite, sandstone
Height 111.8 cm (44 in.)
1996.140

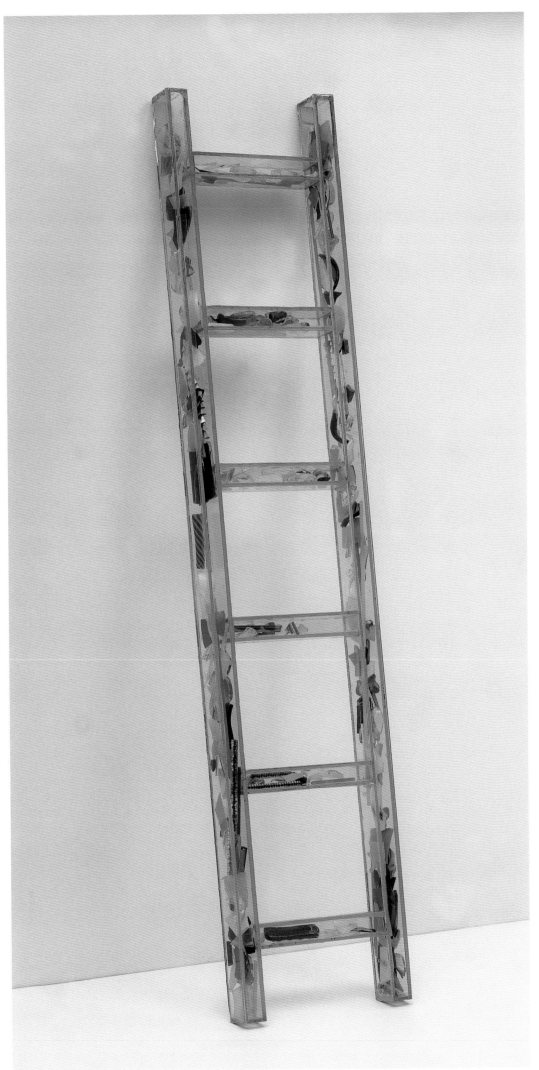

THERMAN STATOM

Ladder
1990–92
Plate glass, found objects
Height 152.4 cm (60 in.)
1996.85

70

THERMAN STATOM

Bird Storm
1994–95
Plate glass, found objects, wood
Height 121.9 cm (48 in.)
1996.84

LINO TAGLIAPIETRA

Goccia Vase
1995
Blown glass
Height 71.1 cm (28 in.)
1996.97

72

72

JANUSZ WALENTYNOWICZ

For the Moment
1995
Cast glass, wood
Height 101.6 cm (40 in.)
1996.100

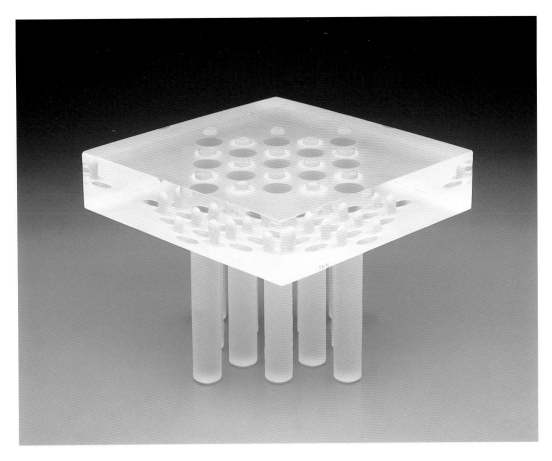

73

STEVEN WEINBERG

#481201
1984
Cast glass
Height 15.2 cm (6 in.)
1996.93

74

MEREDITH WENZEL

Untitled
1982
Blown glass
Height 22.9 cm (9 in.)
1996.148

JON M. WOLFE

Retiform 3
1983
Blown glass
Height 20.3 cm (8 in.)
1996.155

76

ANN WOLFF

Bowl
1980
Blown glass
Height 12.7 cm (5 in.)
1996.161

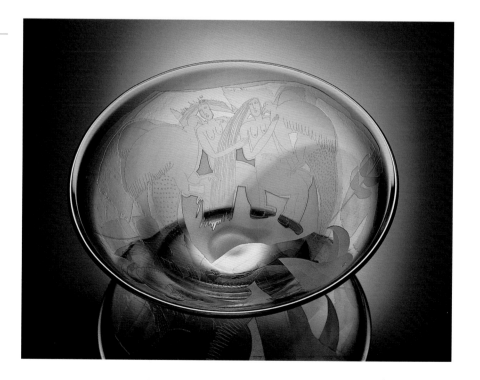

77

CZESŁAW ZUBER

The Beast or *La Bête*
1987
Fabricated glass
Height 33 cm (13 in.)
1996.151

78

TOOTS ZYNSKY

Silk Bowl from the African
Dream series
1984
Glass threads
Height 10.2 cm (4 in.)
1996.122

Selected public collections and references are listed.

HERB BABCOCK

American, born 1946

Education: Cleveland Institute of Art, B.F.A. 1969; Cranbrook Academy of Art, Bloomfield Hills, Mich., M.F.A. 1973

Related Professional Experience: Faculty, Center for Creative Studies, College of Art and Design, Detroit, 1974–present

Collections:

Columbus Museum of Art, Ohio

Detroit Institute of Arts

Erstes Wiener Glasmuseum der Fa. Lobmeyr, Vienna

Glasmuseum Frauenau, Germany

Kunstsammlungen der Veste Coburg, Germany

Museum für Kunst und Gewerbe, Hamburg

Muskegon Museum of Art, Mich.

Toledo Museum of Art, Ohio

University of Michigan–Dearborn

References:

Farmington Hills 1994

Seattle 1993

GARY BEECHUM

American, born 1955

Education: University of Wisconsin–Madison, B.S. 1979

Related Professional Experience: Visiting artist, J. & L. Lobmeyr and Sons, Vienna, 1978; assistant to Harvey Littleton, Spruce Pine, N.C., 1980–85; independent artist, 1985–present

Collections:

Asheville Art Museum, N.C.

Erstes Wiener Glasmuseum der Fa. Lobmeyr, Vienna

Galerie Internationale du Verre, Biot, France

Glasmuseum Ebeltoft, Denmark

Glasmuseum Frauenau, Germany

High Museum of Art, Atlanta

Kunstmuseum Düsseldorf

Milwaukee Art Museum

Mint Museum of Art, Charlotte, N.C.

Musée du Verre, Liège, Belgium

References:

Beechum 1984

Hampson 1984

Hampson 1985

Kanazawa 1992

Tokyo 1992

HOWARD BEN TRÉ

American, born 1949

Education: Portland State University, Oreg., B.S.A. 1978; Rhode Island School of Design, Providence, M.F.A. 1980

Related Professional Experience: Independent artist, 1980–present

Collections:

Albright-Knox Art Gallery, Buffalo

American Craft Museum, New York

Brooklyn Museum of Art

Corning Museum of Glass, N.Y.

Detroit Institute of Arts

Hirshhorn Museum and Sculpture Garden, Smithsonian Institution, Washington, D.C.

Kalamazoo Institute of Arts, Mich.

Metropolitan Museum of Art, New York

Renwick Gallery of the National Museum of American Art, Smithsonian Institution, Washington, D.C.

Toledo Museum of Art, Ohio

References:

Corning 1979

Frantz and Spillman 1990

Hawley 1997

Klein 1989

Koplos 1991

Milwaukee 1993

Morristown 1992

Providence 1993

Richmond 1995

Toledo 1995

ZOLTÁN BOHUS

Hungarian, born 1941

Education: Hungarian Academy of Applied Arts, Budapest, M.A. 1966

Related Professional Experience: Hungarian Academy of Applied Arts, 1966–present

Collections:

Bakonyi Múzeum, Veszprém, Hungary

Corning Museum of Glass, N.Y.

Iparművészeti Múzeum, Budapest

Kunstmuseum Düsseldorf

Kunstsammlungen der Veste Coburg, Germany

Magyar Nemzeti Galéria, Budapest

Musée de la Verrerie, Sars-Poteries, France

Musée des Beaux-Arts et de la Céramique, Rouen

Museum Bellerive, Zürich

Museum für Angewandte Kunst, Hamburg

References:

Farmington Hills 1994

Klein 1989

Nagy 1981

Ricke 1990

Seattle 1997

CURTISS R. BROCK

American, born 1961

Education: Goddard College, Plainfield, Vt., B.A. 1984; University of Illinois at Champaign-Urbana, M.F.A. 1994

Related Professional Experience: Faculty, Pilchuck Glass School, Stanwood, Wash., summers 1985–96; Appalachian Center for Crafts, Smithville, Tenn., 1989–present

Collections:

American Craft Museum, New York

Birmingham Museum of Art, Ala.

Charles A. Wustum Museum of Fine Arts, Racine, Wis.

Chrysler Museum of Art, Norfolk, Va.
Corning Museum of Glass, N.Y.
Detroit Institute of Arts
Glasmuseum Ebeltoft, Denmark
J. B. Speed Art Museum, Louisville, Ky.
Muskegon Museum of Art, Mich.
Saint Louis Art Museum
References:
Frantz 1989
Hampson 1984
Hampson 1985
Hampson and Boone 1987
Sapporo 1988

JANE BRUCE
American, born 1961
Education: Leicester Polytechnic, England, diploma of art and design 1970; Royal College of Art, London, M.A. 1973
Related Professional Experience: Faculty, The Glasshouse, London, 1973–79; School of Furniture and Design, Buckinghamshire College, England, 1973–79; Ohio University, Athens, 1981–85; New York University, 1985–93; UrbanGlass (New York Experimental Glass Workshop), New York, 1991–94; Canberra School of Art, Australian National University, 1994–present
Collections:
Broadfield House Glass Museum, Kingswinford, England
Charles A. Wustum Museum of Fine Arts, Racine, Wis.
Crafts Council of Great Britain, London
Detroit Institute of Arts
Kunstsammlungen der Veste Coburg, Germany
Los Angeles County Museum of Art
Museum für Kunsthandwerk, Frankfurt am Main
Victoria and Albert Museum, London
References:
Hampson 1989
Lynn 1997
Perrault 1996

KENNETH CARDER
American, born 1955
Education: Bowling Green State University, Ohio, 1975–80
Related Professional Experience: Studio assistant to William Bernstein, Celo, N.C., 1981–84; artist-in-residence, Penland School of Crafts, N.C., 1984–88; independent artist, 1988–present
Collections:
Asheville Art Museum, N.C.
Detroit Institute of Arts
Glasmuseum Ebeltoft, Denmark
Mint Museum of Art, Charlotte, N.C.
References:
Hampson 1984
Seattle 1992a

WILLIAM CARLSON
American, born 1950
Education: Cleveland Institute of Art, B.F.A. 1973; Alfred University, New York, M.F.A. 1976
Related Professional Experience: Faculty, University of Illinois at Champaign-Urbana, 1976–present
Collections:
Columbus Museum of Art, Ohio
Corning Museum of Glass, N.Y.

Detroit Institute of Arts
Hokkaido Museum of Modern Art, Sapporo
Kyoto Museum of Modern Art
Los Angeles County Museum of Art
Metropolitan Museum of Art, New York
Milwaukee Art Museum
Musée des Arts Décoratifs, Lausanne
Saint Louis Art Museum
References:
Beeh 1988
Carlson 1985
Detroit 1984
Klein 1989
Smith and Lucie-Smith 1986

SYDNEY CASH
American, born 1941
Education: Wayne State University, Detroit, B.S. 1965
Related Professional Experience: Faculty, Brooklyn Museum Art School, 1972–75; Pratt Institute, Brooklyn, 1973–74; Pilchuck Glass School, Stanwood, Wash., summer 1986; independent artist, 1975–present
Collections:
Corning Museum of Glass, N.Y.
Morris Museum, Morristown, N.J.
Musée des Arts Décoratifs, Lausanne
Museum of Modern Art, New York
References:
DiNoto 1982
Hollister 1981
Talaba 1983

JOSÉ CHARDIET
American, born 1956
Education: Southern Connecticut State University, New Haven, B.A. 1980; Kent State University, Ohio, M.F.A. 1983
Related Professional Experience: Artist-in-residence, Kent State University, Ohio, 1985; faculty, University of Illinois at Champaign-Urbana, 1991–present
Collections:
Corning Museum of Glass, N.Y.
High Museum of Art, Atlanta
Musée des Arts Décoratifs, Lausanne
Museum of American Glass at Wheaton Village, Millville, N.J.
Yokohama Museum of Art, Japan
References:
Hampson and Boone 1987
Heineman 1988
Oakland 1986
Seattle 1993

DALE CHIHULY
American, born 1941
Education: University of Washington, Seattle, B.A. 1965; University of Wisconsin–Madison, M.S. 1967; Rhode Island School of Design, Providence, M.F.A. 1968
Related Professional Experience: Faculty, Rhode Island School of Design, Providence, 1969–79; founded Pilchuck Glass School, Stanwood, Wash., 1971; independent artist, 1980–present
Collections:
American Craft Museum, New York
Cooper-Hewitt National Design Museum, Smithsonian Institution, New York

Corning Museum of Glass, N.Y.
Glasmuseum Ebeltoft, Denmark
Metropolitan Museum of Art, New York
Museum für Kunsthandwerk, Frankfurt am Main
Museum of Modern Art, New York
Renwick Gallery of the National Museum of American Art,
    Smithsonian Institution, Washington, D.C.
Victoria and Albert Museum, London
Whitney Museum of American Art, New York
References:
Beaumont 1993
Chihuly 1994
Daytona Beach 1993
Honolulu 1992
Kuspit 1997
Los Angeles 1980
Paris 1986
Ricke 1991
Seattle 1992b
Tokyo 1990

DAN DAILEY
American, born 1947
Education: Philadelphia College of Art, B.F.A. 1969; Rhode Island
School of Design, Providence, M.F.A. 1972
Related Professional Experience: Designer, Steuben Glass, New
York, 1984–85; Fenton Art Glass Company, Williamstown, W.V.,
1984–85; faculty, Massachusetts College of Art, Boston, 1989–present
Collections:
American Craft Museum, New York
Corning Museum of Glass, N.Y.
Detroit Institute of Arts
Los Angeles County Museum of Art
Metropolitan Museum of Art, New York
Musée des Arts Décoratifs, Lausanne
National Gallery of Victoria, Melbourne
National Museum of Modern Art, Kyoto
Royal Ontario Museum, Toronto
Toledo Museum of Art, Ohio
References:
Chambers 1988
Cohen and Cohen 1983
Dailey 1985
Dailey 1986
Hawley 1997
Hunter-Steibel 1981
Klein 1989
Norden 1988
Onorato 1981
Ruby 1981

MAXWELL DAVIS
American, born 1947
Education: Southern Illinois University, Carbondale, B.A. 1970;
University of Michigan, Ann Arbor, M.F.A. 1973
Related Professional Experience: Faculty, Center for Creative
Studies, Detroit, 1973–present
Collections:
Detroit Institute of Arts
High Museum of Art, Atlanta
References:
Farmington Hills 1994

STEVEN DEVRIES
American

STEPHEN DEE EDWARDS
American, born 1954
Education: San José State University, Calif., B.A. 1978; Illinois State
University, Normal, M.F.A. 1980
Related Professional Experience: Faculty, Alfred University,
N.Y., 1988–present
Collections:
Asheville Art Museum, N.C.
Corning Museum of Glass, N.Y.
Glasmuseum Ebeltoft, Denmark
Hokkaido Museum of Modern Art, Sapporo
Mint Museum of Art, Charlotte, N.C.
Musée des Arts Décoratifs, Lausanne
Renwick Gallery of the National Museum of American Art,
    Smithsonian Institution, Washington, D.C.
Saint Louis Art Museum
Württembergisches Landesmuseum Stuttgart
Yokohama Museum of Art, Japan
References:
Hampson 1984
Klein 1989

BOHUMIL ELIÁŠ
Czech, born 1937
Education: Střední uměleckoprůmyslová škola sklářská, Železný
Brod, Czechoslovakia, 1954–57; Vysoká škola Uměleckoprůmyslová,
Prague, 1957–63
Related Professional Experience: Independent artist
Collections:
Kunstgewerbemuseum, Düsseldorf
Moravské muzeum v Brně, Czech Republic
Musée des Arts Décoratifs, Lausanne
Musée des Arts Décoratifs, Paris
Museo del Vidrio, Monterrey, Mexico
Museum Jan Van Der Togt, Amstelveen, The Netherlands
Muzeum skla a bižuterie, Jablonec nad Nisou, Czech Republic
Uměleckoprůmyslové muzeum, Prague
Yokohama Museum of Art, Japan
References:
Hošková 1994
Petrová 1988

MICHAEL GLANCY
American, born 1950
Education: University of Denver, B.F.A. 1973; Rhode Island
School of Design, Providence, B.F.A. 1977, M.F.A. 1980
Related Professional Experience: Faculty, Denver Free
University, 1971; Pilchuck Glass School, Stanwood, Wash., summers
1982–88; faculty, artist-in-residence, Rhode Island School of Design,
Providence, 1982–93; independent artist, 1993–present
Collections:
Art Gallery of Western Australia, Perth
Corning Museum of Glass, N.Y.
Detroit Institute of Arts
Glasmuseum Ebeltoft, Denmark
Los Angeles County Museum of Art
Metropolitan Museum of Art, New York
Musée des Arts Décoratifs, Lausanne
Musée des Arts Décoratifs, Paris

Toledo Museum of Art, Ohio
Victoria and Albert Museum, London
References:
DiNoto 1982
Hammel 1989
Hampson 1984
Klein 1991
Klein 1995
McTwigan 1990

PAVEL HLAVA
Czech, born 1924
Education: Střední uměleckoprůmyslová škola sklářská, Železný Brod, Czechoslovakia, 1938–42; Vysoká škola Uměleckoprůmyslová, Prague, 1942–48
Related Professional Experience: Employed at Central Art Center for the Glass and Fine Ceramics Industries, Prague, 1957–58; Institute of Interior and Fashion Design, Prague, 1959–85
Collections:
Art Gallery of New South Wales, Sydney
Corning Museum of Glass, N.Y.
Glasmuseum Ebeltoft, Denmark
Kunstsammlungen der Veste Coburg, Germany
Musée des Arts Décoratifs, Lausanne
Museum Bellerive, Zürich
Museum Boymans-van Beuningen, Rotterdam
Uměleckoprůmyslové muzeum, Prague
Victoria and Albert Museum, London
Yokohama Museum of Art, Japan
References:
Petrová 1995

W. STEPHEN HODDER
American, born 1951
Education: Tyler School of Art, Temple University, Elkins Park, Penn., B.F.A. 1979; University of Minnesota, Minneapolis, M.F.A. 1982
Related Professional Experience: Faculty, University of Minnesota, Minneapolis, 1987–88; independent artist, 1988–present
Collections:
American Craft Museum, New York
Charles A. Wustum Museum of Fine Arts, Racine, Wis.
Detroit Institute of Arts
High Museum of Art, Atlanta
Milwaukee Art Museum
Museum of American Glass at Wheaton Village, N.J.
References:
Hampson 1986
Hampson 1989
Hampson and Boone 1987
Heineman 1988

DAVID HOPPER
American, born 1946
Education: San José State University, Calif., M.F.A. 1969
Related Professional Experience: Owner, operator, designer, Orient & Flume Art Glass, Chico, Calif., 1985–present
Collections:
Chrysler Museum of Art, Norfolk, Va.
Corning Museum of Glass, N.Y.
Glasmuseum Ebeltoft, Denmark
Glasmuseum Frauenau, Germany

Hokkaido Museum of Modern Art, Sapporo
Huntington Museum of Art, W.V.
J. B. Speed Art Museum, Louisville, Ky.
Musée des Arts Décoratifs, Lausanne
National Gallery of Victoria, Melbourne
References:
Waggoner 1989

DAVID R. HUCHTHAUSEN
American, born 1951
Education: University of Wisconsin–Wausau, B.F.A. 1974; Illinois State University, Normal, M.F.A. 1977; Hochschule für Angewandte Kunst, Vienna, Fulbright Scholar 1977–78
Related Professional Experience: Assistant to Harvey Littleton, Spruce Pine, N.C., 1973; faculty, Appalachian Center for Crafts, Smithville, Tenn., 1981–present
Collections:
American Craft Museum, New York
Corning Museum of Glass, N.Y.
Detroit Institute of Arts
Erstes Wiener Glasmuseum der Fa. Lobmeyr, Vienna
Glasmuseum Ebeltoft, Denmark
Glasmuseum Frauenau, Germany
Hokkaido Museum of Modern Art, Sapporo
Kunstsammlungen der Veste Coburg, Germany
Metropolitan Museum of Art, New York
Toledo Museum of Art, Ohio
References:
Frantz and Spillman 1990
Hampson 1989
Hampson and Boone 1987
Heineman 1988
Klein 1989
Manhart and Manhart 1987
Sapporo 1991
Silberman 1987

ULRICA HYDMAN-VALLIEN
Swedish, born 1938
Education: National College of Art, Craft, and Design, Stockholm, 1958–61
Related Professional Experience: Designer, Kosta Boda AB, Sweden, 1972–present; faculty, Pilchuck Glass School, Stanwood, Wash., summers 1981–88
Collections:
Corning Museum of Glass, N.Y.
Glasmuseum Ebeltoft, Denmark
Hokkaido Museum of Modern Art, Sapporo
Kunstmuseum Düsseldorf
Kunstsammlungen der Veste Coburg, Germany
Musée des Arts Décoratifs, Paris
Nationalmuseum, Stockholm
National Museum of Modern Art, Tokyo
Powerhouse Museum, Sydney
Victoria and Albert Museum, London
References:
Ricke 1990
Sapporo 1991
Stensman 1990

KREG KALLENBERGER
American, born 1950
Education: University of Tulsa, B.F.A. 1972, M.A. 1974
Related Professional Experience: Faculty, University of Tulsa, 1979–84; independent artist, 1985–present
Collections:
American Craft Museum, New York
Corning Museum of Glass, N.Y.
Detroit Institute of Arts
Indianapolis Museum of Art
High Museum of Art, Atlanta
Hokkaido Museum of Modern Art, Sapporo
Musée des Arts Décoratifs, Lausanne
Museum of Fine Arts, Boston
Pilkington Glass Museum, Saint Helens, England
Toledo Museum of Art, Ohio
References:
Farmington Hills 1994
Toledo 1993
Tulsa 1986

JOEY KIRKPATRICK
American, born 1952
Education: University of Iowa, Iowa City, B.F.A. 1975; Iowa State University, Ames, 1978–79; Pilchuck Glass School, Stanwood, Wash., summer 1979
Related Professional Experience: Faculty, University of Illinois at Champaign-Urbana, 1981–82; Pilchuck Glass School, Stanwood, Wash., summers 1981–83, 1986–90, 1991–present; Haystack Mountain School of Crafts, Deer Isle, Maine, 1994; independent artist, 1983–present
Collections:
Corning Museum of Glass, N.Y.
Detroit Institute of Arts
Glasmuseum Ebeltoft, Denmark
Hokkaido Museum of Modern Art, Sapporo
Leigh Yawkey Woodson Art Museum, Wausau, Wis.
Metropolitan Museum of Art, New York
Musée des Arts Décoratifs, Lausanne
Renwick Gallery of the National Museum of American Art, Smithsonian Institution, Washington, D.C.
Seattle Art Museum
Toledo Museum of Art, Ohio
References:
Biskeborn 1990
Frantz 1989
Frantz and Spillman 1990
Heineman 1988
Klein 1989
Miller 1989
Sapporo 1991

JON KUHN
American, born 1949
Education: Washburn University, Topeka, Kans., B.F.A. 1972; Virginia Commonwealth University, Richmond, M.F.A. 1978
Related Professional Experience: Independent artist, 1978–present
Collections:
Corning Museum of Glass, N.Y.
Detroit Institute of Arts
Glasmuseum Ebeltoft, Denmark
High Museum of Art, Atlanta

J. B. Speed Art Museum, Louisville, Ky.
Metropolitan Museum of Art, New York
Mint Museum of Art, Charlotte, N.C.
Musée des Arts Décoratifs, Lausanne
Museum für Kunst und Gewerbe, Hamburg
White House Collection, Washington, D.C.
References:
Boca Raton 1996
Byrd 1995a
Hampson and Boone 1987
Hickory 1992
Hollister 1988
Klein 1989
McLease 1994
Monroe 1995
Traverse City 1993

DOMINICK LABINO
American, 1910–87
Education: Carnegie Institute of Technology, Pittsburgh, 1930–34; Toledo Museum School of Design, Ohio
Related Professional Experience: Vice president, director of research and development, Johns-Manville Fiber Glass, Alton, Ill., 1950s–65
Collections:
Art Institute of Chicago
Cleveland Museum of Art
Corning Museum of Glass, N.Y.
Kunstgewerbemuseum, Berlin
Kunstmuseum Düsseldorf
Metropolitan Museum of Art, New York
Museum für Kunsthandwerk, Frankfurt am Main
Museum für Kunst und Gewerbe, Hamburg
Toledo Museum of Art, Ohio
Victoria and Albert Museum, London
References:
Beard 1968
Cullowhee 1982
Florian 1966
Tokyo 1981
Toledo 1974

ETIENNE LEPERLIER
French, born 1952
Education: Studied *pâte de verre* with his grandfather, F. Decorchemont
Related Professional Experience: Independent artist, 1980–present
Collections:
Cooper-Hewitt National Design Museum, Smithsonian Institution, New York
Kunstsammlungen der Veste Coburg, Germany
Musée Ariana, Geneva
Musée de la Verrerie, Sars-Poteries, France
Musée des Arts Décoratifs, Paris
Musée d'Unterlinden, Colmar, France
References:
Klein 1989
Sapporo 1985

MARVIN LIPOFSKY
American, born 1938
Education: University of Illinois at Champaign-Urbana, B.F.A.

1962; University of Wisconsin–Madison, M.S., M.F.A. 1964
Related Professional Experience: Faculty, University of
Wisconsin–Madison, 1964; University of California, Berkeley,
1964–72; California College of Arts and Crafts, Oakland, 1967–87
Collections:
Corning Museum of Glass, N.Y.
Detroit Institute of Arts
Hokkaido Museum of Modern Art, Sapporo
Kunstsammlungen der Veste Coburg, Germany
Musée des Arts Décoratifs, Paris
Museum Boymans-van Beuningen, Rotterdam
Museum für Kunst und Gewerbe, Hamburg
Museum of Decorative Arts, Sofia, Bulgaria
Nationaal Glasmuseum, Leerdam, The Netherlands
Stedelijk Museum, Amsterdam
References:
Porges 1991
Treib 1968
White 1991

HARVEY K. LITTLETON
American, born 1922
Education: Brighton School of Art, England, 1945; University of
Michigan, Ann Arbor, B.D. 1947; Cranbrook Academy of Art,
Bloomfield Hills, Mich., M.F.A. 1951
Related Professional Experience: Faculty, Toledo Museum
School, Toledo Museum of Art, Ohio, 1949–51; University of
Wisconsin–Madison, 1951–77; independent artist, 1978–present
Collections:
American Craft Museum, New York
Cooper-Hewitt National Design Museum, Smithsonian Institution,
    New York
Corning Museum of Glass, N.Y.
Detroit Institute of Arts
Glasmuseum Ebeltoft, Denmark
Hokkaido Museum of Modern Art, Sapporo
Kunstsammlungen der Veste Coburg, Germany
Metropolitan Museum of Art, New York
Museum of Modern Art, New York
Österreichisches Museum für Angewandte Kunst, Vienna
References:
Atlanta 1984
Byrd 1980
DiNoto 1982
Ebeltoft 1989
Hunter-Steibel 1981
Koplos 1984
Kyoto 1982
Littleton 1971
Littleton 1988
Littleton 1993

JOHN LUEBTOW
American, born 1944
Education: California Lutheran College, Thousand Oaks
B.A. 1967; University of California, Los Angeles, M.A. 1969,
M.F.A. 1976
Related Professional Experience: Worked with Harvey Littleton,
Spruce Pine, N.C., 1973, 1975; independent artist, 1971-present
References:
Hampson 1989
Hampson and Boone 1987

Heineman 1988
Lockwood 1988
Moody 1987
Van Deventer 1988

MÁRIA LUGOSSY
Hungarian, born 1950
Education: Hungarian Academy of Applied Arts, Budapest, degree
in goldsmithing 1973, M.A. 1975
Related Professional Experience: Independent artist, 1975–present
Collections:
British Museum, London
Corning Museum of Glass, N.Y.
Glasmuseum Ebeltoft, Denmark
Glasmuseum Frauenau, Germany
Kunstmuseum Düsseldorf
Kunstsammlungen der Veste Coburg, Germany
Musée des Arts Décoratifs, Lausanne
Musée des Arts Décoratifs, Paris
Suntory Museum of Art, Tokyo
Yokohama Museum of Art, Japan
References:
Frank and Gulian 1992
Halasi 1996
Leoffler 1986
Nagy 1981

FLORA C. MACE
American, born 1949
Education: Plymouth State College, N.H., B.S. 1972; University
of Illinois at Champaign-Urbana, M.F.A. 1976
Related Professional Experience: Faculty, Pilchuck Glass School,
Stanwood, Wash., summers 1981–83, 1986–90; Haystack Mountain
School of Crafts, Deer Isle, Maine, 1985, 1994; independent artist,
1977–present
Collections:
Corning Museum of Glass, N.Y.
Detroit Institute of Arts
Glasmuseum Ebeltoft, Denmark
Hokkaido Museum of Modern Art, Sapporo
Leigh Yawkey Woodson Art Museum, Wausau, Wis.
Metropolitan Museum of Art, New York
Musée des Arts Décoratifs, Lausanne
Renwick Gallery of the National Museum of American Art,
    Smithsonian Institution, Washington, D.C.
Seattle Art Museum
Toledo Museum of Art, Ohio
References:
Biskeborn 1990
Frantz 1989
Frantz and Spillman 1990
Heineman 1988
Klein 1989
Miller 1989
Sapporo 1991

PAUL MANNERS
American, born 1946
Education: Harvard College, Cambridge, Mass., B.A. 1967;
University of California, Santa Cruz, 1968–69
Related Professional Experience: Independent artist, 1972–present

KLAUS MOJE

German, born 1936

Education: Journeyman's certificate, training as glass cutter and grinder in family workshop Glasschleiferel Hugo Moje, Hamburg, 1952–55; Staatliche Glasfachschule, Hadamar, Germany, master's certificate, 1957–59

Related Professional Experience: Faculty, Canberra School of Art, Australian National University, 1982–91; independent artist, 1992–present

Collections:

Cooper-Hewitt National Design Museum, Smithsonian Institution, New York

Corning Museum of Glass, N.Y.

Detroit Institute of Arts

Hokkaido Museum of Modern Art, Sapporo

Kunstgewerbemuseum, Berlin

Kunstsammlungen der Veste Coburg, Germany

Metropolitan Museum of Art, New York

National Gallery of Australia, Canberra

Toledo Museum of Art, Ohio

Victoria and Albert Museum, London

References:

Anderson 1984

Edwards 1990

Edwards 1995

Hollister 1984–1985

Ioannou 1995

Joppien 1996

Ricke 1991

82 WILLIAM MORRIS

American, born 1957

Education: California State University, Chico, 1975–76; Central Washington University, Ellensburg, 1977–78

Related Professional Experience: Independent artist, 1978–present

Collections:

American Craft Museum, New York

Corning Museum of Glass, N.Y.

Hokkaido Museum of Modern Art, Sapporo

Los Angeles County Museum of Art

Metropolitan Museum of Art, New York

Musée des Arts Décoratifs, Paris

Museum für Kunst und Gewerbe, Hamburg

Toledo Museum of Art, Ohio

University of Michigan–Dearborn

Victoria and Albert Museum, London

References:

Biskeborn 1990

Blonston 1993

Blonston 1996

Failing 1993

Hall 1977

Kangas 1994

Netzer 1993b

Sapporo 1994

Seattle 1989

SHINICHI MURO

Japanese, born 1949

Education: Kanazawa College of Art, Japan, 1973

Related Professional Experience: Faculty, Kanazawa College of Art, 1973–present

Collections:

Corning Museum of Glass, N.Y.

Glasmuseum Ebeltoft, Denmark

Suntory Museum of Art, Tokyo

References:

Ebeltoft 1997

Farmington Hills 1994

Frantz 1989

JAY MUSLER

American, born 1949

Education: California College of Arts and Crafts, Oakland, 1968–71

Related Professional Experience: Glassblower, Maslach Art Glass, Greenbrae, Calif., 1972–81; faculty, Pilchuck Glass School, Stanwood, Wash., summer 1985; Renwick Gallery of the National Museum of American Art, Smithsonian Institution, Washington, D.C., 1988, 1992; independent artist, 1993–present

Collections:

Corning Museum of Glass, N.Y.

Detroit Institute of Arts

Hokkaido Museum of Modern Art, Sapporo

J. B. Speed Art Museum, Louisville, Ky.

Los Angeles County Museum of Art

Milwaukee Art Museum

Musée des Arts Décoratifs, Lausanne

Museum of American Glass at Wheaton Village, Millville, N.J.

Toledo Museum of Art, Ohio

References:

Frantz 1989

Hammel 1988

Hollister 1985

Marks 1992

Porges 1995

Sapporo 1982

Sapporo 1985

Sapporo 1991

JOEL PHILIP MYERS

American, born 1934

Education: Parsons School of Design, New York, 1951–54; Alfred University, N.Y., B.F.A., M.F.A. 1960–63

Related Professional Experience: Director of design, Blenko Glass Company, Milton, W.V., 1963–70; faculty, Illinois State University, Normal, 1970–96

Collections:

American Craft Museum, New York

Corning Museum of Glass, N.Y.

Detroit Institute of Arts

Erstes Wiener Glasmuseum der Fa. Lobmeyr, Vienna

Hokkaido Museum of Modern Art, Sapporo

Kunstgewerbemuseum, Berlin

Kunstsammlungen der Veste Coburg, Germany

Los Angeles County Museum of Art

Museum Boymans-van Beuningen, Rotterdam

Toledo Museum of Art, Ohio

References:

Ebeltoft 1993

Frantz 1989

Hollister 1983

Klein 1989

Los Angeles 1988

Monroe 1995
Save 1988

ROBERT PALUSKY
American, born 1942
Education: University of Wisconsin–Superior, B.F.A. 1967;
Rochester Institute of Technology, N.Y., M.F.A. 1969
Related Professional Experience: Faculty, Kirkland College,
Clinton, N.Y., 1969–77; Hamilton College, Clinton, N.Y., 1977–
present
Collections:
American Craft Museum, New York
Corning Museum of Glass, N.Y.
Glasmuseum Ebeltoft, Denmark
Hokkaido Museum of Modern Art, Sapporo
Musée des Arts Décoratifs, Lausanne
Museum of Fine Arts, Boston
Museum of Modern Art, New York
References:
Chambers 1990
Sapporo 1988

MICHAEL PAVLIK
Czech, born 1941
Education: College of Arts and Crafts, Prague, M.A. 1963
Related Professional Experience: Faculty and artist-in-residence,
Hartwick College, Oneonta, N.Y., 1974–85; independent artist,
1986–present
Collections:
American Craft Museum, New York
Carnegie Museum of Art, Pittsburgh
Charles A. Wustum Museum of Fine Arts, Racine, Wis.
Cooper-Hewitt National Design Museum, Smithsonian Institution,
   New York
Corning Museum of Glass, N.Y.
Hokkaido Museum of Modern Art, Sapporo
Musée des Arts Décoratifs, Lausanne
Museum für Kunst und Gewerbe, Hamburg
Toledo Museum of Art, Ohio
References:
Seattle 1992a
Toledo 1993

MARK PEISER
American, born 1938
Education: Purdue University, Lafayette, Ind., 1957; Illinois
Institute of Technology, Chicago, B.S. 1961; DePaul University,
Chicago, music degree 1967
Related Professional Experience: Faculty, Penland School of
Crafts, N.C., 1968–70, 1972, 1979; Pilchuck Glass School,
Stanwood, Wash., summer 1975; School for American Craftsmen,
Rochester Institute of Technology, N.Y., 1976–77; Haystack
Mountain School of Crafts, Deer Isle, Maine, 1982; independent
artist, 1983–present
Collections:
Art Institute of Chicago
Birmingham Museum of Art, Ala.
Chrysler Museum of Art, Norfolk, Va.
Cooper-Hewitt National Design Museum, Smithsonian Institution,
   New York
Corning Museum of Glass, N.Y.
High Museum of Art, Atlanta

Mint Museum of Art, Charlotte, N.C.
Museum of American Glass at Wheaton Village, Millville, N.J.
National Museum of American Art, Smithsonian Institution,
   Washington, D.C.
References:
Byrd 1979
Byrd 1989
Byrd 1995b
Seattle 1993

STEPHEN ROLFE POWELL
American, born 1952
Education: Centre College, Danville, Ky., B.A. 1974; Louisiana
State University, Baton Rouge, M.F.A. 1983
Related Professional Experience: Faculty, Centre College,
Danville, Ky., 1983–present
Collections:
Birmingham Museum of Art, Ala.
Hermitage Museum, Saint Petersburg, Russia
Huntsville Museum of Art, Ala.
Mobile Museum of Art, Ala.
References:
Farmington Hills 1994
Hawley 1997

DAMIAN PRIOUR
American, born 1949
Education: University of Texas at Austin, B.A. 1972; University of
California, Berkeley, design studies 1977
Related Professional Experience: Faculty, Pilchuck Glass School,
Stanwood, Wash., summers, 1991, 1993; Centro de Art Vidrio,
Monterrey, Mexico, 1992; independent artist, 1993–present
Collections:
Boca Raton Museum of Art, Fla.
Columbus Museum of Art, Ohio
Corning Museum of Glass, N.Y.
References:
Hampson 1989
Heineman 1988
Priour 1988

CLIFFORD RAINEY
British, born 1948
Education: Hornsey College of Art, London, 1968–69; North East
London Polytechnic School of Sculpture, 1969–71; Royal College
of Art, London, 1971–73
Related Professional Experience: Independent artist, 1973–present
Collections:
Art Gallery of Western Australia, Perth
Arts Council Gallery, Belfast
Arts Council of Great Britain, England
Kunstsammlungen der Veste Coburg, Germany
Municipal Gallery, Dublin
Musée des Arts Décoratifs, Lausanne
Ulster Museum, Belfast
Victoria and Albert Museum, London
References:
Klein 1989
Tokyo 1980

RICHARD Q. RITTER, JR.
American, born 1940

Education: Art School of the Society of Arts and Crafts, Detroit, B.A. 1968; Penland School of Crafts, N.C., 1971
Related Professional Experience: Faculty, Center for Creative Studies, Detroit, 1968–70; faculty and artist-in-residence, Bloomfield Art Association, Birmingham, Mich., 1969–72; Penland School of Crafts, N.C., 1972–77, 1981, 1985, 1988, 1990, 1992–93, 1995; independent artist, 1971–present
Collections:
American Craft Museum, New York
Chrysler Museum of Art, Norfolk, Va.
Corning Museum of Glass, N.Y.
Detroit Institute of Arts
Eastern Michigan University, Ypsilanti
Mint Museum of Art, Charlotte, N.C.
Museum of American Glass at Wheaton Village, Millville, N.J.
Saint Louis Art Museum
White House Collection, Washington, D.C.
References:
Byrd 1996
Hampson 1984

GINNY RUFFNER
American, born 1952
Education: University of Georgia, Athens, B.F.A. 1974, M.F.A. 1975
Related Professional Experience: Independent artist, 1975–present
Collections:
American Craft Museum, New York
Cooper-Hewitt National Design Museum, Smithsonian Institution, New York
Corning Museum of Glass, N.Y.
Detroit Institute of Arts
Hokkaido Museum of Modern Art, Sapporo
Kunstmuseum Düsseldorf
Metropolitan Museum of Art, New York
Musée des Arts Décoratifs, Lausanne
Renwick Gallery of the National Museum of American Art, Smithsonian Institution, Washington, D.C.
Toledo Museum of Art, Ohio
References:
Andrearin 1990
Biskeborn 1990
Kangas 1991
Marks 1990
Maxwell 1988
Miller 1990
New York 1990
Waggoner 1988
Washington 1991
Yood 1995

KARL SCHANTZ
American, born 1944
Education: Rochester Institute of Technology, N.Y., M.F.A. 1969
Related Professional Experience: Faculty, Sheridan College, Mississauga, Ontario, 1974–80; Ontario College of Art, Toronto, 1980–97; independent artist, 1998–present
Collections:
Corning Museum of Glass, N.Y.
Decorative Arts Museum, Vancouver
Museum of Man, Ottawa
National Museum of Modern Art, Tokyo
Sandwich Glass Museum, Mass.

References:
Farmington Hills 1994
Hampson 1984
Klein 1989
Tokyo 1981

THOMAS SCOON
American, born 1961
Education: Illinois State University, Normal, B.F.A. 1988; Massachusetts College of Art, Boston, M.F.A. 1990
Related Professional Experience: Independent artist, 1990–present
Collections:
Detroit Institute of Arts
Glasmuseum Ebeltoft, Denmark
References:
Farmington Hills 1994
Scoon 1994

THERMAN STATOM
American, born 1953
Education: Pilchuck Glass School, Stanwood, Wash., summer 1973; Rhode Island School of Design, Providence, B.F.A. 1974; Pratt Institute of Art and Design, Brooklyn, M.F.A. 1980
Related Professional Experience: Faculty, University of Rhode Island, Kingston, 1976; Pratt Fine Arts Center, Seattle, 1980–81; Colorado Mountain College, Aspen, 1983; University of California, Los Angeles, 1983–85; Pilchuck Glass School, Stanwood, Wash., summers 1984–86; Pitzer College, Claremont, Calif., 1985; independent artist, 1985–present
Collections:
American Craft Museum, New York
Corning Museum of Glass, N.Y.
Detroit Institute of Arts
High Museum of Art, Atlanta
Los Angeles County Museum of Art
Musée des Arts Décoratifs, Paris
Oakland Museum of California
Toledo Museum of Art, Ohio
References:
Chambers 1994
Kangas 1996
Los Angeles 1980
Nzegwu 1994

LINO TAGLIAPIETRA
Italian, born 1934
Education: Apprentice, Archimede Seguso Glass Factory, Murano, Italy, 1946–56
Related Professional Experience: Master glassblower, Galliano Ferro Glass Factory, Murano, 1956–66; worked at Venini Glass Factory, Murano, 1966–68; La Murrina Glass Factory, Murano, 1968–76; head designer and master glassblower, Effetre International, Murano, 1976–88; faculty, Pilchuck Glass School, Stanwood, Wash., summers 1979, 1983, 1985, 1987, 1992; Haystack Mountain School of Crafts, Deer Isle, Maine, 1986–87, 1990; independent artist, 1989–present
Collections:
Corning Museum of Glass, N.Y.
Glasmuseum Ebeltoft, Denmark
Hokkaido Museum of Modern Art, Sapporo
Mint Museum of Art, Charlotte, N.C.
Musée des Arts Décoratifs, Lausanne

Musée des Arts Décoratifs, Paris
Museum Boymans-van Beuningen, Rotterdam
Seattle Art Museum
Victoria and Albert Museum, London
References:
Glowen 1997
Klein 1996
Marquis 1997–98
Sarpellon 1994

JANUSZ WALENTYNOWICZ
Polish, born 1956
Education: Skolen for Brugskunst, Copenhagen, 1978–82; Illinois
State University, Normal, 1982–88
Related Professional Experience: Independent artist, 1988–present
Collections:
American Craft Museum, New York
Arkansas Arts Center, Little Rock
Corning Museum of Glass, N.Y.
Glasmuseum Ebeltoft, Denmark
References:
Chicago 1996
Copeland 1995
Netzer 1993a

STEVEN WEINBERG
American, born 1954
Education: Alfred University, N.Y., B.F.A. 1976; Rhode Island
School of Design, Providence, M.F.A. 1979
Related Professional Experience: Independent artist, 1976–present
Collections:
American Craft Museum, New York
Corning Museum of Glass, N.Y.
Detroit Institute of Arts
Hokkaido Museum of Modern Art, Sapporo
Kunstmuseum Düsseldorf
Los Angeles County Museum of Art
Metropolitan Museum of Art, New York
Musée des Arts Décoratifs, Paris
Renwick Gallery of the National Museum of American Art,
   Smithsonian Institution, Washington, D.C.
Toledo Museum of Art, Ohio
References:
Farmington Hills 1994
Smith and Lucie-Smith 1986
Tokyo 1981
Toledo 1993

MEREDITH WENZEL
American, born 1951
Education: Tyler School of Art, Temple University abroad, Rome,
1971–72; Tyler School of Art, Temple University, Philadelphia,
B.F.A. 1973, M.F.A. 1975
Related Professional Experience: Independent artist, 1975–present
Collections:
Corning Museum of Glass, N.Y.
Glasmuseum Frauenau, Germany
References:
Frantz 1989
Hampson 1984

JON M. WOLFE
American, born 1955
Education: Parkland College, Champaign, Ill., A.A. 1976;
University of Illinois at Champaign-Urbana, B.F.A. 1978, M.F.A.
1984; Pilchuck Glass School, Stanwood, Wash., summer 1981
Related Professional Experience: Faculty, University of Illinois at
Champaign-Urbana, 1985–86; Parkland College, Champaign, Ill.,
1994–97; University of Illinois at Champaign-Urbana, 1997–present
Collections:
Corning Museum of Glass, N.Y.
High Museum of Art, Atlanta
Hunter Museum of American Art, Chattanooga
Huntington Museum of Art, W.V.
Museum of American Glass at Wheaton Village, Millville, N.J.
Yokohama City Museum, Japan
References:
Frantz 1989
Hampson 1984
Hampson 1985
Hampson 1989

ANN WOLFF
Swedish, born 1937
Education: Hochschule für Gestaltung, Ulm, Germany, 1956–59
Related Professional Experience: Designer, Pukesbergs Glasbruk,
Nybro, Sweden, 1960–64; Kosta Boda AB, Sweden, 1964–78;
faculty, Pilchuck Glass School, Stanwood, Wash., summers 1977–85;
Art-Academie, Hamburg, 1993–present
Collections:
Corning Museum of Glass, N.Y.
Erstes Wiener Glasmuseum der Fa. Lobmeyr, Vienna
Hokkaido Museum of Modern Art, Sapporo
Kunstmuseum Düsseldorf
Kunstsammlungen der Veste Coburg, Germany
Metropolitan Museum of Art, New York
Museum Bellerive, Zürich
Nationalmuseum, Stockholm
Stedelijk Museum, Amsterdam
Victoria and Albert Museum, London
References:
Huldt 1993
Tafel 1986
Zerhusen 1990

CZESŁAW ZUBER
Polish, born 1948
Education: Superior School of Arts and Graphics, Wrocław,
Poland, M.A. 1974
Related Professional Experience: Designer, Factory of Art Glass,
Polanica, Poland, 1975–79; freelance designer, Cristallerie Valery
Sthal, France, 1982–83; independent artist, 1983–present
Collections:
Corning Museum of Glass, N.Y.
Hokkaido Museum of Modern Art, Sapporo
Kunstsammlungen der Veste Coburg, Germany
Musée des Arts Décoratifs, Lausanne
Musée des Arts Décoratifs, Paris
Musée d'Unterlinden, Colmar, France
Museo Nacional de Cerámica, Valencia, Spain
Museum Bellerive, Zürich
Museum für Kunst und Gewerbe, Hamburg
National Museum of Modern Art, Tokyo

References:
Bloch-Dermant 1986
Paris 1987
Paris 1989

TOOTS ZYNSKY
American, born 1951
Education: Rhode Island School of Design, Providence, B.F.A. 1973
Related Professional Experience: Assisted Dale Chihuly in founding of Pilchuck Glass School, Stanwood, Wash., 1971–73; faculty, New York Experimental Workshop, 1980–81; Parsons School of Design, New York, 1981–82; artist-in-residence, University of California, Los Angeles, 1984; independent artist, 1985–present
Collections:
American Craft Museum, New York
Cooper-Hewitt National Design Museum, Smithsonian Institution, New York
Corning Museum of Glass, N.Y.
Glasmuseum Ebeltoft, Denmark
Metropolitan Museum of Art, New York
Museum of Modern Art, New York
Muskegon Museum of Art, Mich.
National Gallery of Victoria, Melbourne
Toledo Museum of Art, Ohio
White House Collection, Washington, D.C.

References:
Bester 1995
Klein 1989
Mual 1995
Sapporo 1988
Seattle 1992b
Sinz 1987
Toledo 1993
Venice 1995

STEPHEN DEE EDWARDS,
Lattice Physalia and *Ocean Dancer*
(no. 18), 1983, detail

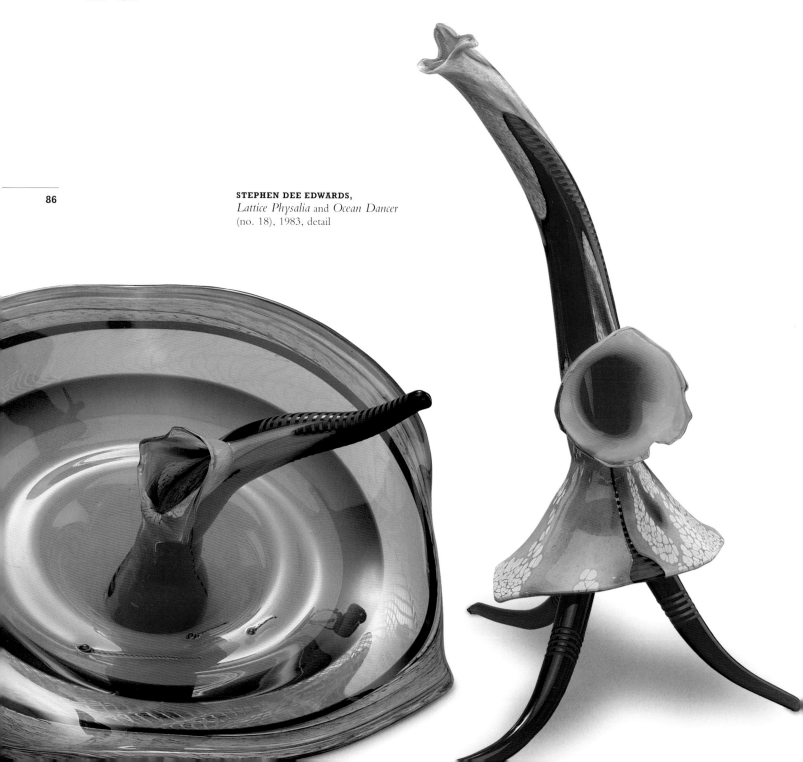

Bibliography

In addition to references to books and articles cited in the essay and artists' biographies, the bibliography includes material intended to provide a wider background on the studio glass movement.

ANDERSON 1984
Anderson, N. "A Symphony in Glass." *Craft Australia*, no. 4 (1984): 49–54.

ANDREARIN 1990
Andrearin, C. "Ginny Ruffner." *La Revue de la Céramique et du Verre* (spring 1990): cover story.

ASHEVILLE 1994
Dancing in a Garden of Light: Contemporary Glass from the Collection of Isaac and Sonia Lusk. Asheville, N.C.: Asheville Art Museum, exh. cat., 1994.

ATLANTA 1984
Harvey K. Littleton: A Retrospective Exhibition. Atlanta: High Museum of Art, exh. cat., 1984.

BEARD 1968
Beard, G. *Modern Glass.* England, 1968.

BEAUMONT 1993
Chihuly alla macchia: From the George R. Stroemple Collection. Beaumont, Tex.: Art Museum of Southeast Texas, exh. cat., 1993.

BEECHUM 1984
Beechum, G. "Portfolio." *American Craft* (April/May 1984): 25.

BEEH 1988
Beeh, W. *Bildwerke in Glas.* Darmstadt, Germany: Hessisches Landesmuseum, exh. cat., 1988.

BESTER 1995
Bester, J.-C. "Toots Zynsky." *La Revue de la Céramique et du Verre* (January/February 1995): 32–39.

BISKEBORN 1990
Biskeborn, S. *Artists at Work: Twenty-Five Glassmakers, Ceramists, and Jewelers.* Seattle, 1990.

BLOCH-DERMANT 1986
Bloch-Dermant, J. "Poetic Expressions in Glass by Czeslaw Zuber." *Neues Glas*, no. 1 (January/March 1986): 29–33.

BLONSTON 1993
Blonston, G. "Through a Glass Artfully." *Art & Antiques* (December 1993): 58–63.

BLONSTON 1996
_____. *William Morris: Artifacts/Glass.* New York, 1996.

BOCA RATON 1996
Jon Kuhn. Boca Raton, Fla.: Habatat Galleries, exh. cat., 1996.

BYRD 1979
Byrd, J. F. "Mark Peiser: Glass as a Magic Lens." *American Craft* (August 1979): 32–35.

BYRD 1980
_____. "Harvey Littleton: Pioneer in American Studio Glass." *American Craft* (February 1980): 2–7.

BYRD 1989
_____. "Mark Peiser." *New Work* (spring 1989): 8–13.

BYRD 1995A
_____. "Jon Kuhn: Radiant Vision." *American Craft* (October/November 1995): cover, 70–73.

BYRD 1995B
_____. "The North Carolina Glass Community." *The Glass Art Society Journal* (1995): 26–30.

BYRD 1996
_____. "Richard Ritter: Thinking in the Language of Glass." *American Craft* (August/September 1996): 48–49.

CARLSON 1985
Carlson, W. "Chicago Board Optics Exchange: Optional Refractions." *American Craft* 45 (February/March 1985): 28–29.

CHAMBERS 1988
Chambers, K. S. "Dan Dailey: A Designing Character." *New Work* (1988): 11–19.

CHAMBERS 1990
_____. "Robert Palusky: A Thinking Man's Artist." *Glass Work*, no. 4 (January 1990): 3–12.

CHAMBERS 1994
_____. "On The Brink: Therman Statom." *Neues Glas* (April 1994): 8–19.

CHAMBERS 1995
_____. "Robert Carlson." *Glass Magazine*, no. 61 (winter 1995): 50.

CHAMBERS 1996
_____. "Fifth Annual International Figurative Invitational." *Glass Magazine*, no. 63 (summer 1996): 57.

CHAMBERS 1997
_____. "When Glass is Not a Glass . . . Vitreous Sculpture." *American Style* (spring 1997): 30–39.

CHICAGO 1996
Art of Janusz Walentynowicz. Chicago: Polish Museum of America, Marx-Saunders Gallery, exh. cat., 1996.

CHIHULY 1994
Chihuly, D. *Chihuly Baskets.* Seattle, exh. cat., 1994.

CLEVELAND 1997
Glass Today: American Studio Glass from Cleveland Collections. Cleveland: Cleveland Museum of Art, exh. cat., 1997.

COHEN AND COHEN 1983
Cohen, S., and J. Cohen. "Dan Dailey." *Art Papers* 7, no. 2 (March/April 1983): 21.

COPELAND 1995
Copeland, B. M. "Interview: Janus Walentynowicz." *Glass Focus* 9 (April/May 1995): 1.

CORNING 1979
New Glass: A Worldwide Survey. Corning, N.Y.: Corning Museum of Glass, exh. cat., 1979.

CULLOWHEE 1982
Dominick Labino: Glass Retrospective. Cullowhee, N.C.: Chelsea Gallery, exh. cat., 1982.

CULLOWHEE 1990
North Carolina Glass '90. Cullowhee, N.C.: Chelsea Gallery, exh. cat., 1990.

DAILEY 1985
Dailey, D. "Artist's Statement." *New Work,* nos. 21/22 (winter/spring 1985): 24.

DAILEY 1986
_____. "The Artist's Statement on Design." *The Glass Art Society Journal* (1986): 39–40.

DAYTONA BEACH 1993
Chihuly: Form from Fire. Daytona Beach, Fla.: Museum of Arts and Sciences, exh. cat., 1993.

DETROIT 1984
Contemporary American Glass. Detroit: Habatat Galleries, exh. cat., 1984.

DINOTO 1982
DiNoto, A. "New Masters of Glass." *Connoisseur Magazine* (August 1982): 22–24.

DOUGLAS 1992
Douglas, M. "Chihuly Sweep Stakes: The Venetians, Tutti Putti, Niijima Floats, Glassmaster." *Art Papers* (November/December 1992): 6–9.

EBELTOFT 1989
Littleton-Fujita Exhibition. Ebeltoft, Denmark: Glasmuseum Ebeltoft, exh. cat., 1989.

EBELTOFT 1993
Joel Philip Myers. Ebeltoft, Denmark: Glasmuseum Ebeltoft, exh. cat., 1993.

EBELTOFT 1997
Made in Japan. Ebeltoft, Denmark: Glasmuseum Ebeltoft, exh. cat., 1997.

EDWARDS 1990
Edwards, G. "Like an Oriental Calzedonio: Neues glas von Klaus Moje." *Neues Glas,* no. 3 (1990): 202–9.

EDWARDS 1995
_____. *Klaus Moje Glass: A Retrospective Exhibition.* Melbourne, Australia: National Gallery of Victoria, exh. cat., 1995.

FAILING 1993
Failing, P. "William Morris Glass Remains." *American Craft* (February/March 1993): 49–51.

FARMINGTON HILLS 1994
The Twenty-Second Annual International Glass Invitational. Farmington Hills, Mich.: Habatat Galleries, exh. cat., 1994.

FLORIAN 1966
Florian, R. "Dominick Labino: The Color of Glass Dictates Form." *Craft Horizons* (July/August 1966): 29–31.

FRANK AND GULIAN 1992
Frank, J., and T. Gulian. *Mária Lugossy: Enclaves.* N.p., 1992.

FRANTZ 1989
Frantz, S. K. *Contemporary Glass: A World Survey from the Corning Museum of Glass.* New York, 1989.

FRANTZ AND SPILLMAN 1990
Frantz, S. K., and J. S. Spillman. *Masterpieces of American Glass.* New York, 1990, 82–83.

GLOWEN 1997
Glowen, R., et al. "Lino Tagliapietra." *The Glass Art Society Journal* (1997): 8–14.

HALASI 1996
Halasi, R. "Under the Spell of Glass." *Neues Glas,* no. 1 (1996): 26–33.

HALL 1977
Hall, J. *Tradition and Change: The New American Craftsman.* New York, 1977.

HAMMEL 1988
Hammel, L. "An Apocalyptic Art." *American Craft* (October/November 1988): cover, 26–29.

HAMMEL 1989
_____. *Shadow and Substance: The Art of Michael Glancy.* New York: Heller Gallery, exh. cat., 1989.

HAMPSON 1984
Hampson, F. *Glass: State of the Art.* Huntington Woods, Mich., 1984.

HAMPSON 1985
_____. *Insight: A Collector's Guide to Contemporary American Glass.* Huntington Woods, Mich., 1985.

HAMPSON 1986
_____. *Works: In Glass.* Farmington Hills, Mich.: Habatat Galleries, exh. cat., 1986.

HAMPSON 1989
_____. *Glass: State of the Art II.* Huntington Woods, Mich., 1989.

HAMPSON AND BOONE 1987
Hampson, F. C., and T. J. Boone. *25 Years, Glass as an Art Medium,* Lathrup Village, Mich., 1987.

HAWLEY 1997
Hawley, H. H. *Glass Today: American Studio Glass from Cleveland Collections.* Cleveland: Cleveland Museum of Art, exh. cat., 1997.

HEINEMAN 1988
Heineman, B. W., Sr. *Contemporary Glass: A Private Collection.* Chicago, 1988.

HICKORY 1992
Jon Kuhn. Hickory, N.C.: Hickory Museum of Art, exh. cat., 1992.

HOLLISTER 1981
Hollister, P. "Theater in Glass." *American Craft* (October 1981): 26–29.

HOLLISTER 1983
_____. "Joel Philip Myers' Glass: A Peaceful Way of Working." *Neues Glas* (March 1983): 128–33.

HOLLISTER 1984–85
Hollister, P. "Klaus Moje." *American Craft* (December 1984–January 1985): 18–22.

HOLLISTER 1985
_____. "Jay Musler Painted Glass: The Face of Anger." *Neues Glas* (January 1985): 12–19.

HOLLISTER 1988
_____. "Jon Kuhn & Carol Cohen." *Neues Glas*, no. 4 (1988): 281–87.

HONOLULU 1992
Chihuly Courtyards. Honolulu: Honolulu Academy of Arts, 1992.

HOŠKOVÁ 1994
Hošková, S. *Bohumil Eliáš: Glass, Paintings, Drawings (Sklo, Obrazy, Kresby)*. Prague, 1994.

HULDT 1993
Huldt, Å. "The Designer and the Artist." *American Craft* (April/May 1993): 38–41.

HUNTER-STEIBEL 1981
Hunter-Steibel, P. "Contemporary Art Glass: An Old Medium Gets a New Look." *Art News* (summer 1981): 130–35.

IOANNOU 1995
Ioannou, N. *Australian Studio Glass: The Movement, Its Makers and Their Art*. Roseville East, Australia, 1995.

JONES 1993
Jones, R. "Opera for Ten Voices." *The Glass Art Society Journal* (1993): 35–40.

JOPPIEN 1996
Joppien, R. D. "Klaus Moje." *Neues Glas*, no. 1 (1996): 34–37.

KANAZAWA 1992
International Exhibition of Glass Kanazawa '92. Kanazawa, Japan: Kanazawa Chamber of Commerce, exh. cat., 1992.

KANGAS 1991
Kangas, M. "Unravelling Ruffner." *Glass Magazine*, no. 43 (spring 1991): 20–29.

KANGAS 1994
_____. "William Morris." *Glass Magazine*, no. 55 (1994): 22–29.

KANGAS 1995
_____. "Glass Art." *Art News* (January 1995): 51–78.

KANGAS 1996
_____. "Therman Statom." *Glass Magazine*, no. 65 (winter 1996): 30–32.

KANGAS 1997A
_____. "Dreisbach's Encyclopedia of Glass." *Glass Magazine*, no. 69 (winter 1997): 48–51.

KANGAS 1997B
_____. "Ginny Ruffner." *Glass Magazine*, no. 66 (spring 1997): 52.

KLEIN 1989
Klein, D. *Glass: A Contemporary Art*. New York, 1989.

KLEIN 1991
_____. *Michael Glancy-Interaction 1991*. Basel: Galerie von Bartha, exh. cat., 1991.

KLEIN 1995
_____. *Constellations: An Alternative Galaxy*. Basel: Galerie von Bartha, exh. cat., 1995.

KLEIN 1996
_____. "Lino Tagliapietra." *Neues Glas*, no. 2 (1996): 26–33.

KOPLOS 1984
Koplos, J. "Considering the Past." *American Craft* (August/September 1984): 41–44.

KOPLOS 1986
_____. "World Glass Now." *American Craft* (February/March 1986): 10–17.

KOPLOS 1991
_____. "Howard Ben Tré at Charles Cowles." *Art in America*, no. 79 (December 1991): 112–13.

KUSPIT 1997
Kuspit, D. *Chihuly*. New York, 1997.

KYOTO 1982
Contemporary Studio Glass: An International Collection. Kyoto: National Museum of Modern Art, exh. cat., 1982.

LEOFFLER 1986
Leoffler, R. "Mária Lugossy: Glass Sculpture." *Arts Review* 38, no. 3 (November 21, 1986).

LITTLETON 1971
Littleton, H. *Glassblowing: A Search for Form*. New York, 1971.

LITTLETON 1988
_____. "Studio Glass Movement: Yesterday, Today, Tomorrow." *Neues Glas*, no. 4 (October/December 1988): 260–61.

LITTLETON 1993
_____. "Glass: A Potential for Prints." *The Glass Art Society Journal* (1993): 78–80.

LOCKWOOD 1988
Lockwood, K. "Rhymes in Light." *Craft Arts Magazine*, no. 12 (May/June 1988): 89–91.

LOS ANGELES 1980
Four Leaders in Glass: Dale Chihuly, Richard Marquis, Therman Statom, Dick Weiss. Los Angeles: Craft and Folk Art Museum, exh. cat., 1980.

LOS ANGELES 1988
Joel Philip Myers. Los Angeles: Kuland/Summers Gallery, exh. cat., 1988.

LYNN 1997
Lynn, M. D. *Masters of Contemporary Glass: Selections from the Glick Collection*. Indianapolis: Indianapolis Museum of Art, exh. cat., 1997.

MANHART AND MANHART 1987
Manhart, M., and T. Manhart. *The Eloquent Object: The Evolution of American Art in Craft Media Since 1945*. Tulsa: Philbrook Museum of Art, exh. cat., 1987.

MARKS 1990
Marks, B. "Field of Dreams." *American Craft* (June/July 1990): 47–49.

MARKS 1992
_____. "The Brinkmanship of Jay Musler." *Glass Magazine* (fall 1992): cover, 20–27.

MARQUIS 1997–98
Marquis, R. "Lino Tagliapietra." *American Craft* (December 1997–January 1998): 41–45.

MAXWELL 1988
Maxwell, J. "Ruffner." *New Work*, no. 34 (summer 1988): 8–11.

MCLEASE 1994
McLease, J. "A Touch of Glass." *Winston-Salem Magazine* (August/September 1994).

MCTWIGAN 1990
McTwigan, M. "Balancing Order and Chaos." *Glass Magazine*, no. 42 (1990): cover, 20–29.

MILLER 1989

Miller, B. "Double Vision." *American Craft* (October 1989): 40–45.

MILLER 1990

_____. "Ginny Ruffner." *Glasswork*, no. 6 (August 1990): cover.

MILWAUKEE 1993

Tiffany to Ben Tré: A Century of Glass. Milwaukee: Milwaukee Art Museum, exh. cat., 1993.

MILWAUKEE 1997

Recent Glass Sculpture: A Union of Ideas. Milwaukee: Milwaukee Art Museum, exh. cat., 1997.

MONROE 1995

Monroe, M. *The White House Collection of American Crafts.* New York, exh. cat., 1995.

MOODY 1987

Moody, J. "Fusing Artist Explores Inner Qualities of Glass." *Glass Art Magazine* (November/December 1987): 24–27.

MORRISTOWN 1992

Glass: From Ancient Craft to Contemporary Art, 1962–1992 and Beyond. Morristown, N.J.: Morris Museum, exh. cat., 1992.

MUAL 1995

Mual, M. "Order in Chaos." *Glas en Keramik* (September/October 1995): 38–42.

NAGY 1981

Nagy, I. "Exercises in Time & Space." *Neues Glas*, no. 3 (1981): 89–95.

NETZER 1993A

Netzer, S. "Janus A. Walentynowicz." *Neues Glas*, no. 4 (1993): 8–17.

NETZER 1993B

_____. "William Morris." *Neues Glas* (March 1993): 12–21.

NEW YORK 1989

Craft Today U.S.A. New York: American Craft Museum, exh. cat., 1989.

NEW YORK 1990

Explorations: The Aesthetic of Excess. New York: American Craft Museum, exh. cat., 1990.

NEW YORK 1996A

American Images: The SBC Collection of Twentieth-Century American Art. New York, 1996.

NEW YORK 1996B

Studio Glass in the Metropolitan Museum of Art. New York: Metropolitan Museum of Art, exh. cat., 1996.

NORDEN 1988

Norden, L. "A Rainbow in the Dark." *New Work*, no. 35 (fall 1988): 20–23.

NZEGWU 1994

Nzegwu, N. "Living in a Glass House, Passing through Glass: The Art of Therman Statom, James Watkins and John Dowell, Jr." *International Review of African-American Art II*, no. 2 (1994): 44–51.

OAKLAND 1986

Contemporary American and European Glass from the Saxe Collection. Oakland, Calif.: Oakland Museum, exh. cat., 1986.

ONORATO 1981

Onorato, R. J. "Dan Dailey—Directions in Glass." *American Craft* (February/March 1981): 24–27, 74–75.

PARIS 1986

Dale Chihuly: Objets de verre. Paris: Musée des Arts Décoratifs, exh. cat., 1986.

PARIS 1987

Les Bêtes: Czeslaw Zuber. Paris: Galerie DM Sarver, exh. cat., 1987.

PARIS 1989

Czeslaw Zuber: Don't Be Distracted! Paris: Galerie DM Sarver, exh. cat., 1989.

PERRAULT 1996

Perrault, J. "Jane Bruce: The Search for a Place." *Urban Glass Quarterly* (1996).

PETROVÁ 1988

Petrová, S. "Bohumil Eliás: Optik und Kinetik." *Neues Glas* (1988): 103–7.

PETROVÁ 1995

_____. *Pavel Hlava.* Prague: Uméleckoprúmyslové Muzeum, exh. cat., 1995.

PORGES 1991

Porges, M. "Marvin Lipofsky—Artist and Educator." *Neues Glas* (1991): 8–15.

PORGES 1995

_____. "Jay Musler." *Glass & Art*, no. 9 (1995): cover, 35–49.

PRIOUR 1988

Priour, D. "Portfolio." *American Craft* (April/May 1988): 60.

PROVIDENCE 1993

Howard Ben Tré: New Work. Providence, R.I.: Brown University, exh. cat., 1993.

RICHMOND 1995

Howard Ben Tré: Recent Sculpture. Richmond, Va.: Marsh Art Gallery, University of Richmond, with Cleveland Center for Contemporary Art, exh. cat., 1995.

RICKE 1990

Ricke, H. *Neues Glas in Europa: 50 Künstler—50 Konzepte.* Düsseldorf: Kunstmuseum, exh. cat., 1990.

RICKE 1991

_____. *Dale Chihuly-Klaus Moje.* Ebeltoft, Denmark: Glasmuseum, exh. cat., 1991.

RUBY 1981

Ruby, K. "Exhibitions, Invitational Sampler." *Art Week* (May 1981): 1.

SAINT LOUIS 1995

Made in America; Ten Centuries of American Art. Saint Louis: Saint Louis Art Museum, exh. cat., 1995.

SAPPORO 1982

World Glass Now '82. Sapporo: Hokkaido Museum of Modern Art, exh. cat., 1982.

SAPPORO 1985

World Glass Now '85. Sapporo: Hokkaido Museum of Modern Art, exh. cat., 1985.

SAPPORO 1988

World Glass Now '88. Sapporo: Hokkaido Museum of Modern Art, exh. cat., 1988.

SAPPORO 1991
World Glass Now '91. Sapporo: Hokkaido Museum of Modern Art, exh. cat., 1991.

SAPPORO 1994
World Glass Now '94. Sapporo: Hokkaido Museum of Art, exh. cat., 1994.

SARPELLON 1994
Sarpellon, G. *Lino Tagliapietra.* Venice, 1994.

SAVE 1988
Save, Colette. "Joel Philip Myers: Glass Vertigo." *L'Atelier* (May 1988).

SCOON 1994
Scoon, T. "Thomas Scoon." *New Art Examiner* 22 (October 1994): 35–36.

SEATTLE 1989
William Morris: Artifact and Art. Seattle, 1989.

SEATTLE 1992A
"A Cultural Odyssey," "Personal Mythologies: Veil of Illusion," and "Czechoslovakia: Over the Hurdles." *The Glass Art Society Journal* (Seattle, 1992).

SEATTLE 1992B
Dale Chihuly: Installations 1964–1992. Seattle: Seattle Art Museum, exh. cat., 1992.

SEATTLE 1993
"Panel: Casting Techniques." *The Glass Art Society Journal* (Seattle, 1993): 120–25.

SEATTLE 1997
Richard Marquis Objects. Seattle: Seattle Art Museum, exh. cat., 1997.

SILBERMAN 1987
Silberman, R. "Huchthausen: Controlled Fragments." *American Craft* (September 1987): 54–59.

SINZ 1987
Sinz, D. "Toots Zynsky, Glas für Glas, Color for Color." *Neues Glas* (October/December 1987): 276–79.

SMITH 1991
Smith, John P. *Osler's Crystal for Royalty and Rajahs.* London, 1991.

SMITH 1993
Smith, Jan. "Pulling Cane: Millefiori, an Ancient Art in Contemporary Form," *The Glass Art Society Journal* (1993): 81–84.

SMITH AND LUCIE-SMITH 1986
Smith, P. J., and E. Lucie-Smith, *Craft Today: Poetry of the Physical.* New York: American Craft Museum, exh. cat., 1986.

STENSMAN 1990
Stensman, *M. Ulrica Hydman-Vallien.* Älmhult, Sweden, 1990.

TAFEL 1986
Tafel, V. "Discoveries and Changes: New Works by Ann Wolff." *Neues Glas,* no. 4 (1986): 258–64.

TALABA 1983
Talaba, M. "Profile: Sydney Cash." *Glass Magazine* 10, no. 1 (January 1983): 15–19.

TOKYO 1980
Contemporary Glass: Europe & Japan. Tokyo: National Museum of Modern Art, exh. cat., 1980.

TOKYO 1981
Contemporary Glass: Australia, Canada, U.S.A. & Tokyo. Tokyo: National Museum of Modern Art, exh. cat., 1981.

TOKYO 1990
Dale Chihuly: Japan 1990. Tokyo: Japan Institute of Arts and Crafts, exh. cat., 1990.

TOKYO 1992
Survey of Glass in the World, vol. 6, *Contemporary Glass.* Tokyo, 1992.

TOLEDO 1974
Dominick Labino: A Decade of Craftsmanship, 1964–1974. Toledo: Toledo Museum of Art, exh. cat., 1974.

TOLEDO 1993
Contemporary Crafts and the Saxe Collection. Toledo: Toledo Museum of Art, exh. cat., 1993.

TOLEDO 1995
Toledo Treasures: Selections From the Toledo Museum of Art. Toledo: Toledo Museum of Art, exh. cat., 1995.

TRAVERSE CITY 1993
Jon Kuhn. Traverse City, Mich.: Dennos Museum, exh. cat., 1993.

TREIB 1968
Treib, E. M. "Marvin Lipofsky: Just Doing His Glass Thing." *Craft Horizons* (September/October 1968): 16–19.

TULSA 1986
3 Series: Kallenberger in Glass. Tulsa: Philbrook Art Center, exh. cat., 1986.

VAN DEVENTER 1988
Van Deventer, M. J. "John Gilbert Luebtow." *Art Gallery International* (July/August 1988): cover, 28–32.

VENICE 1995
Toots Zynsky. Venice: D'Arte & Divetro, exh. cat., 1995.

WAGGONER 1988
Waggoner, S. "This Is Lampworking?" *Glass Art* (December 1988): cover, 5–8.

WAGGONER 1989
———. "Glass Art People." *Glass Art* (September/October 1989): 46–49.

WASHINGTON 1991
Ginny Ruffner. Washington, D.C.: Maurine Littleton Gallery, exh. cat., 1991.

WAUSAU 1981
Americans in Glass. Wausau, Wisc.: Leigh Yawkey Woodson Art Museum, exh. cat., 1981.

WHITE 1991
White, C. "Marvin Lipofsky: Roving Ambassador of Glass." *American Craft* (October/November 1991): cover, 47–51.

YOOD 1995
Yood, J. "Ginny Ruffner and Steve Kursh." *Glass Magazine,* no. 60 (fall 1995): 28–32.

ZERHUSEN 1990
Zerhusen, K. "Suicide of a Glasshouse." *Neues Glas,* no. 2 (1990): 70–75.